Islam Discourages Polygamy and Divorce A Reality, Not a Myth

Islam Discourages Polygamy and Divorce A Reality, Not a Myth

KHWAJA ABDUL MUNTAQIM

KALPAZ

ISBN: 978-93-5128-174-0

Price: ₹ 490

First Published, 2016

Published by

Kalpaz Publications
C-30, Satyawati Nagar,
Delhi – 110052
E-mail: kalpaz@hotmail.com
Ph.: 9212142040

Printed at: G. Print Process, Delhi

Cataloging in Publication Data—DK
Courtesy: D.K. Agencies (P) Ltd. <docinfo@dkagencies.com>

Muntaqim, Khwaja A. (Khwaja Abdul), author.
Islam discourages polygamy and divorce a reality, not a myth /Khwaja Abdul Muntaqim.
pages cm
Includes bibliographical references.
ISBN 9789351281740

1. Women in Islam. 2. Marriage—Religious aspects—Islam. 3. Muslim women—India—Social conditions. 4. Marriage law— India. 5. Muslim women—Legal status, laws, etc.—India. I. Title.

BP173.4.M86 2016 DDC 297.082 23

Contents

Preface

It is propagated and generally believed that Muslims are a polygamous community believing in plurality of wives and commonly practicing polygamy. Sometimes, it is also propagated that polygamy was unknown to those professing other religions and that Islam is its originator. Fact of the matter is that it is merely a myth or a pre-supposed proposition. An extract from the book 'The Muslim Law of Marriage' (Compiled from the original Arabic authorities) by Al-Haj Mahomed Ullah Ibn S. JUNG, Barrister-at-Law, Lincoln's Inn, and High Court of Allahabad; Professor of Law at the University of Allahabad, reproduced below, presents a different picture and has a different story to tell:

"The Muslim law tolerates polygamy which was customary among the ancient Arabs. It was practised by the Jews and was enjoined in certain cases by the Mosaic law. The 'ancient' Christian Church did not forbid it. The Anabaptists and Bernardino Ochino approved of the institution of plurality of wives. In 1540, Luther consented to the second marriage of Philip the Magnanimous, who married with his wife's approval. Among the tribes of Africa, Australia and the Mormons of America, we find, that polygamy was customary. The Hindu Law did not restrict the number of wives. (The situation has changed after the enactment of the Hindu Marriage Act, 1955 and a provision has also been incorporated in the Indian Penal Code declaring bigamy an offence punishable under the Code.) The monogamous marriage of modern times is the outcome of a slow growth, starting from the state of sexual promiscuity, irregular and temporary unions. However, all the ancient nations did not indulge in polygamy. The Veddas of Ceylon wandered through the forests in monogamous pairs with their wives, children and hunting dogs. The

Romans later on preferred monogamy, and it was a fundamental rule of Roman Law that a man could not have two wives at the same time "*duos uxores eoden tempore habere non-licet.*" The Muslim Law inherited the doctrine of plurality of wives from time immemorial. So many Prophets had married a number of wives. Jacob had Joseph and his brothers born of different wives, the Prophet Solomon had contracted numerous marriages. Abraham the traditional founder of the Quresh Arabs had at least two wives. He left his second wife Hajra and Ismael at Mecca. While in ancient Arabia there was no restriction, as to the number of wives that one could legally marry, Islam limited the number to four, and represented monogamy, as an ideal form of marriage."

V. R. Krishna Iyer, a Former Judge of the Supreme Court of India, has, in his book titled "The Dialectics & Dynamics of Human Rights in India (Yesterday, Today and Tomorrow- P. 129) has rightly said that:

"Quranic injunction has to be understood in the perspective of prevalent unrestricted polygamy and in the context of the battle in which most males perished, leaving many females or orphans and that the Holy prophet himself recognised the difficulty of treating two or more wives with equal justice and, in such a situation, directed that an individual should have only one wife. In short, the Quran enjoined monogamy upon Muslims and departure therefrom as an exception. That is why, in the true spirit of the Quran, a number of Muslim countries have codified the personal law wherein the practice of polygamy has been either totally prohibited or severely restricted."

In order to curb unjustified plural marriages many Muslim/Non-Muslim Countries have framed various laws with regard to Bigamy/ Polygamy.

As regards socio-legal status of Muslim women and their empowerment, they are almost or by and large at the same pedestal at which all other women of the world are. Empowerment of women and removal of inequality between men and women, be it professional inequality, ownership inequality, household inequality, basic facility inequality, mortality inequality, natality inequality, as categorised by Nobel Laureate Amartya Sen, is still a priority global issue. But in a male oriented and male dominated society, they can be the safe players only if their human rights against discrimination in every walk of life and sphere of activity and non-equality, sexual harassment, privacy, domestic violence etc. are fully protected and their right to empowerment, be it economic, social, cultural and political, is not only recognised and highlighted but it is fully enforced and religiously implemented.

Promoting women rights has been a long-term objective of the United Nations. Several conferences have been held not only during the UN sponsored International Women Decade but prior to and thereafter. They have been running from pillar to post to raise their voice against discrimination and non-equality. They had to travel all the way from Mexico in 1975 to Copenhagen in 1980, to Nairobi in 1985 and to Beijing in 1995 where International conventions on women issues were held from time to time.

In different parts of the world male chauvinism in different degrees has led to gender injustice. In some developed countries, too, women were accorded the right to vote very late. They had to launch a determined struggle to secure the right of adult franchise. Even when women secured the right to vote initially they did not receive in the legislatures the recognition they deserved on the basis of their merit and ability. If the social reform programme is to be pursued vigorously, certain attitudinal changes are urgently called for. These comprise change of context, change of relations and change of values. Without such a comprehensive change in the existing value judgments of the present consumerist culture, the battle for gender justice cannot be won.

In these days of globalisation, the global picture of women professing all religions or with a faith of their conviction is quite ignoble and inequitable. Women constitute 50 per cent of the world population, and account for 66 per cent of the work done, but they have only a share of 10 per cent in the world income and own one per cent of the world property. In other words, women continue to be at the receiving end and at a fundamental disadvantage in a male dominated society.

As stated above, it is common knowledge that women have always been at No. 2 vis-a-vis men all over the globe at all fronts—

economic, social, political or even legal. Even many a religious scripture denied them absolute equality and have not treated them at par with males in certain matters, such as, personal liberty, participation in governance, succession and matrimonial matters. As regards Muslim women a good deal may be, sometimes in bad taste, has been said about social status of Muslim women in Islam though their position is not as bad as we suppose. However, it is not as good as it ought to have been. In these days of globalisation, the global picture of women is quite grim and so is the condition of Muslim women, being part of the global family. But certain vested interests give such an image of Muslim women as they are born subordinate and constitute the only class of oppressed women who are secluded and hidden behind the veil but the stories of their revolutionary and heroic deeds are/have been ignored.

As regards socio-legal status of Muslim women, Sir William Markby, has dealt with the subject objectively by referring to both sides of the coin—head and tail, that is, dark & bright:

"The strength of a Mahommedan woman's position is that she has rights of her own, and whatever rights she has she can assert without legal impediment, just as if she were a single woman. The theory of the older Roman law and of English law that the wife during marriage has no independent legal existence, is unknown to the Mahommedan law. She can appear as a suitor in a court of justice against a stranger or against her own husband; she can buy and sell, lend and borrow, give and take as she pleases: of course dealing only with her own property, and being liable for her own transactions. Her property is her own, and if she cannot enjoy it as she pleases, because of her husband's control over her actions, she can, at any rate, keep him away from it. In the case, therefore, of a rich wife and a needy husband the wife may obtain a position of almost complete independence."

Tahir Mahmood has, in his book titled "Muslim Law in India and Abroad", jointly authored with Saif Mahmood, a learned advocate of the Supreme Court of India, has also opined that polygamy was certainly not a creation of Islam-unlimited and unconditional polygamy was rampant in the Arab society in any other part of the world either. Islam tried to restrict it by limiting the permissible number of wives and subjecting that restricted permission to the pre-condition of man's capacity to treat the co-wives absolutely equally. It is very unfortunate that while the Quranic permission for polygamy is conventionally regarded as law, its conditions and restrictions in this regard are seen merely as unenforceable Quranic morality or advisory.

The author has tried to remove all possible doubts regarding divorce and polygamy in Islam through this humble presentation in an objective manner without fear and favour.

H-3, Dharma Apartment, **Khwaja Abdul Muntaqim**
2-IP Extn, Delhi - 110092
em:amkhwaja2007@yahoo.co.in
July, 2015

1

Status of Women in Islam

In these days of globalisation, the global picture of women is quite grim and so is the condition of Muslim women, being part of the global family. But certain vested interests give such an image of Muslim women as they are born subordinate and constitute the only class of oppressed women who are secluded and hidden behind the veil. Contrary to this popular belief, the ground situation has a different story to tell. Real stories of their revolutionary and heroic deeds are spread over hundreds of pages of world history.

Many a GREAT MUSLIM WOMAN have reached appreciable heights and commanded respect because of their qualities of head and heart, their virtues, beauties, truthfulness, generosity, patience, knowledge, learning and other qualities worth emulating not only by Muslim women but by all women irrespective of their personal affiliations and their professing different religions. Many of their qualities may be worth emulating even by non-believers. These historical women and many others are the pivots of Muslim civilisation and they may be the role models that contemporary Muslims as also their champions look up to.

Even in recent years Muslim women have been the Prime Ministers of Pakistan (Benazeer Bhutto), Bangladesh (Sheikh Hasina Wajed) and Mali (Cissé Mariam Kaïdama Sidibé). Similarly, the President of Kosovo, Atife Jahjaga, being the world's youngest female president and her country's first female Muslim president, is another addition to the list. So is the President and Commander-in-Chief of Mauritius Ameena Gurib. Since 1988, Bangladesh, Indonesia, Mali, Pakistan, Kosovo, Kyrgyzstan, Senegal and Turkey have been led by a Muslim woman President or Prime Minister.

Mother's Day is not celebrated in Muslim world on any day. But Imam Zaid Shakir wrote about in this event saying: "Women, like the flowers of spring, adorn our lives and have been chosen by Almighty God to deliver into the world the young souls whose presence marks the regeneration of our family." Many a notable Muslim woman have made valuable contribution in all walks of life and spheres of activities in the contemporary world as also in the past as scholars, jurists, rulers, administrators, social workers, warriors, businesswomen, poets etc. In Women's world history, the following extraordinary Muslim women have made remarkable contributions in their respective fields:

Khadija, the wealthy businesswoman and trader wife of the Prophet, supported him morally and financially during his prophecy. Aisha, his other wife, who disseminated great amount of knowledge acquired from the Prophet, became a great jurist and scholar. Umm Salama acted as her political advisor. Hafsa, daughter of Umar ibn AlKhattab, was entrusted with the first copy of the Quran upon her father's death. Fatima, the prophet's daughter and Nusaiba defended the prophet heroically during the battle of Uhud [The Battle of Uhud was fought on Saturday, March 19, 625 (3 Shawwal, 3 AH in the Islamic calendar) at the valley located in front of Mount Uhud between Muslim community of Medina led by the Prophet Muhammad, and a force led by Abu Sufyan ibn Harb from Mecca, the town from which many of the Muslims had previously emigrated. The Battle of Uhud was the second military encounter between the Meccans and the Muslims, preceded by the Battle of Badr in 624].

Muslim women continued to contribute in every field even in later years. Ashifa bint Abdullah, for example, was the first Muslim woman to be appointed by Caliph Umar ibn AlKhattab as a market inspector and manager. (The term "Caliph" is particularly applied to the successors of Prophet Mohammad). Amra bint Abdurrahman was one of the greatest scholars among the second generation of early Muslims. She was a jurist, a mufti: (a juris consult who notifies the decisions of the Muslim Law, in, or respecting, cases submitted to him; an expounder of Muslim Law) and a hadith (a tradition or narration relating to or describing a saying or an action of Prophet Muhammad) scholar in the time of Ummayyad Caliph Umar ibn Abdul Aziz. Aisha bint Sa'd ibn Abi Waqqass was a jurist and scholar who taught the famous Muslim jurist Imam Malik, the founder of the Maliki school of thought. Sayyida Nafisa, the Prophet's great grand daughter, daughter of Al-Hassan ibn Ali ibn Abi Talib, was a teacher of Islamic jurisprudence whose students travelled from faraway places to learn. One of her students was Imam Shafi'i, another great founder of the Shafi'i school of thought. Another Muslim woman scholar who taught famous Muslim men scholars was Aisha bint Muhammad ibn Abdul Hadi in Damascus (now capital of Syria). Umm Darda was a female scholar who taught at the great Ummayyad mosque in Damascus as well as in Jerusalem. One of her students was Caliph Abdul Malik ibn Marwan himself. A twelfth century woman, Shuhadah bint Ahmad al-Ibrii studied in Baghdad with other scholars and became herself a great scholar of hadith and Islamic jurisprudence.

As philanthropists and benefactors, Muslim women like Queen Zubayda, wife of nineth century Caliph Harun Ar-Rasheed in the Abbasid dynasty, made huge contributions to public works, such as, building wells, guest houses and reservoirs. In addition, Queen Zubayda was also an intellectual, a political thinker and a neutral champion of poets and writers irrespective of their religion/faith, as also of religious scholars. On the Western side of the Arab world, nineth century's Fatima al Fihriyya in Fez, Morocco founded al-Qarawwiyyin mosque. It is now one of the oldest Islamic schools and colleges still working. Another woman who built schools was Banafshaa' ar-Rumiyya of the eleventh century who restored schools, bridges, public housing for homeless women in Baghdad. She had her own school endowment. Besides, Fatima of Cordoba was a tenth century librarian who oversaw 70 public libraries containing 400,000 books. Nana Asma'u of Nigeria was a poet, teacher, scholar, and advisor to her father in nineteenth century. This is not the end of the tunnel; there are many other women who have made similar contributions in different spheres.

Muslim women have also been great rulers and queens. Arwa al-Sulayhi, an eleventh century Yemini noble lady ruled for 71 years. Razia Sultana held the throne in India for four years in the thirteenth century. In central India a family of women rulers ruled Bhopal from 1819 to 1924, the last of whom was Begum Kaikhursau Jahan. Sultan Shahjahan Begum (July 29, 1838 – June 16, 1901) was the Begum of Bhopal (the ruler of the princely state of Bhopal in central India) for two periods: 1844–60 (her mother acting as regent), and secondly, during 1868–1901. This family is known for many public works, such as, railway network, water works, and postal system. Even in independent India, Muslim women have been participating in politics and governance, Najma Heptullah, former Lok Sabha speaker, presently being Minister for Minority Affairs, Government of India and Mohsina Kidwai, the Former Minister and an active Congress worker, Madhubala (Mumtaz Jahan Begum), Meena Kumari (Mahjabeen Bano), Noor Jahan, the great film personalities being only a few selective examples. Women in other Muslim countries like Indonesia, Malaysia, Iran, Turkey and Egypt etc. have been actively participating in all walks of life and spheres of activities.

Despite these big achievements, a class of propagandists presents such a homogenous model of Muslim women as if they are the only backward segment of the global society. It cannot be denied that women all over the globe have yet to achieve equality in all walks of life. Even Hillary Clinton, who ran for Presidentship of the United States in 2008 had admitted the factum of inequality in an election speech.

"I am a woman and, like millions of women, I know there are still barriers and biases out there, often unconscious, and I want to build an America that respects and embraces the potential of every last one of us."

As stated above, this class of propagandists presents a homogenous model of Muslim women though the legislation and implementation of basic tenets differs from one country to the other. In most of the Muslim countries women are at liberty to participate in civil, political, economic, social and cultural life but the biased analysts shall generally quote only such isolated societies where they cannot move freely and cannot wear dresses of their choice and have no right to vote. They will refrain from quoting even casually that Islam gave right of inheritance to women at a time when right of inheritance was not available to most of the women professing other religions.

Hon'ble Mr Justice Rajindar Sachar retired Chief Justice of the Delhi High Court, had also expressed similar views. To quote:

"Historically, Islam had been very liberal and is progressive in granting property rights to women. The fact is that there were no property rights to Hindu women until 1956 when the Hindu Code Bill was passed whereas Islam had granted these rights to Muslim women over 1400 years ago." (The Statesman, Delhi, April 26, 1986.)

"The London Times" dated 9th November, 1993 in its editorial writes:

"As the investigation in the Times on Women and Islam has shown the intellectual clarity and moral certainty of this 1400 years-old faith are proving attractive to many western women disillusioned with the moral relationism of their own culture. Though some are converting to Islam after marrying Pakistani or Bangladeshi men, others are making the leap of faith as an independent act of spiritual self improvement.

In spite of the outrageous indignities which many women suffer in Muslim countries the principles outlined in the Koran are generally sympathetic to their interests, promising them rights over men similar to those of men over women.

The separate spheres marked out for the two sexes by Islam certainly bear little relationship to the notions of gender which have been ushered in by the feminist revolution. But what matters is that many of the women in the West who have taken this unexpected path have done so out of choice rather than familial duty or historic obligation. They have been positively attracted by the sense of sisterhood and community they discover in Islam.

This tentative process of spiritual change suggests that increasing numbers of people are questioning the value system of their own culture. It raises important questions about the state of the Western moral tradition and how it might be fortified. Yet the effect of this (still modest) phenomenon is likely to be positive. The presence of Muslim converts in British society many of them highly educated... can only assist the process of mutual understanding between the two cultures."

The editorial has not been reproduced here just to show that the other side of the coin is also the same. Besides, our purpose is also not to highlight that the Muslim women is at a higher pedestal.

Women constitute 50 per cent of the world's population, and account for 66 per cent of the work done, but they have only a share of ten per cent in the world's income and own one per cent of the world's population. And Muslim women are also a part of this miserable world. Their illiteracy or exploitation (wherever it is) can not be attributed to Islam. Islam expects that all categories of persons—children, women and other vulnerable categories should be treated with compassion. Their plight commensurates with the peculiar conditions and the systems of government/governance there. In different parts of the world male chauvinism in different degrees has led to gender injustice. In some developed countries too women were accorded the right to vote very late. They had to launch a determined struggle to secure the right of adult franchise. Even when women secured the right to vote, initially they did not receive in the Legislatures the recognition they deserved on the basis of their merit and ability. If the social-reform programme is to be pursued vigorously, certain attitudinal changes are urgently called for. These comprise change of context, change of relations and change of values. Without such a comprehensive change in the existing value judgments of the present consumerist culture, the battle for gender justice cannot be won.[1]

Muslim women are also feeling the pinch of gender inequality and gender injustice. Muslim countries are also taking concrete steps for the improvement of social status of Muslim women. But fact of the matter is that the status of women in Islam is one of the most extremely misunderstood and incorrectly portrayed things in western society which we prefer to call the modern world.

The concept of gender equality in Islam is stressed by the non-superiority of either sex over the other. The equality of women in Islam is evident by the unprecedented legal rights given to them under a monotheistic religion as defined in Quran and quoted in other sources of Islamic jurisprudence.

A Muslim woman has the following rights in Islam:—

1. The right and duty to obtain education.
2. The right to have her own independent property.
3. The right to work to earn money if she needs it or wants it. (According to the Quran, a woman's role on earth is not limited only to childbirth. She is required to do as many good deeds as any other man is required to do.)
4. Equality of reward for equal deeds.
5. The right to express her opinion and be heard.
6. The right to provisions from the husband for all her needs and more.
7. The right to negotiate marriage terms of her choice.
8. The right to obtain divorce from her husband.

Sir William Markby, a Former Judge of Calcutta High Court in pre-partition India, has, in his book titled "HINDU AND MAHOMMEDAN LAW" while dealing with the subject of legal status of Muslim women has opined as under at pages 147-148:

A Good deal has been said about the position of a Mahommedan women; and Mahommedans are naturally very anxious to make out that it is not as bad as we suppose. There are, no doubt, social customs which protect her, but still it can hardly be denied that the protection afforded to her by the law against an un-scrupulous husband is undoubtedly insufficient. She is always under the disadvantage that, whereas she is irrevocably bound, he is free to discard her whenever he pleases. Even, therefore, if she desires a divorce she must bring her husband into the humour to grant it, and if she dreads a divorce she must always be on her guard not to offend him. It is only in the very rare case of her being indifferent whether he divorces or not that she can venture to act quite independently.

The strength of a Mahommedan woman's position is that she has rights of her own, and whatever rights she has she can assert without legal impediment, just as if she were a single woman. The theory of the older Roman law and of English law that the wife during marriage has no independent legal existence, is unknown to the Mahommedan law. She can appear as a suitor in a court of justice against a stranger or against her own husband; she can buy and sell, lend and borrow, give and take as she pleases: of course dealing only with her own property, and being liable for her own transactions. Her property is her own, and if she cannot enjoy it as she pleases, because of her husband's control over her actions, she can, at any rate, keep him from it. In the case, therefore, of a rich wife and a needy husband the wife may obtain a position of almost complete in dependence.

In matters regarding divorce, reconciliation etc. Islam has been very logical though propagated otherwise. Even a journalist of Khushwant Singh's stature had in his Malice column appearing in The Hindustan Times while relying on data forming part of a research study undertaken in a Delhi University Institute, mentioned that percentage of divorce cases amongst Muslims is lower than that of majority community in India. Divorce has been permitted in Islam only under compulsive and compelling situations. For the wife whose husband's ill-conduct is the cause for the marriage's near collapse, the Quran offers the following advice:

"If a wife fears cruelty or desertion on her husband's part, there is no blame on them if they arrange an amicable settlement between themselves; and such settlement is the best" (4:128). Besides, the Prophet of Islam has condemned beating of wife or wives. Some

Muslim wives complained to him that their husbands had beaten them. Hearing that, the Prophet categorically stated that:

"Those who do so (beat their wives) are not the best among you" (Abu Dawood).

The Prophet advised one Muslim woman, whose name was Fatimah bithe Prophet and said: Abul Jahm and Mu'awiah have proposed to marry me. The Prophet (by way of advice) said: As to Mu'awiah he is very poor and Abul Jahm is accustomed to beating women" (Muslim).

The Quran instructs Muslim men to be kind to their wives even in cases of lukewarm emotions or feelings of dislike:

"Live with them (your wives) on a footing of kindness and equity. If you dislike them it may be that you dislike something in which Allah has placed a great deal of good" (4:19).

Prophet Muhammad gave a similar instruction:

" A believing man must not hate a believing woman. If he dislikes one of her traits he will be pleased with another" (Muslim).

The Prophet while ordering the wives to be obedient had also declared that the best Muslims are those who are best to their wives: To quote:

"The believers who show the most perfect faith are those who have the best character and the best of you are those who are best to their wives" (Tirmidthi).

And further a famous Hadis is mentioned in Muslim:

'The world and all things in it are valuable; but the most valuable thing in the world is a virtuous woman.

9. The right to keep her own money she is not responsible to maintain any relations under normal situation.
10. The right to get sexual satisfaction from her husband.
11. Custody of their children after divorce.

12. Fair treatment to widows :

Widows and divorcees have the freedom to marry whomever they choose. There is no stigma attached to divorce or widowhood in the Quran.

"When you divorce women and they fulfill their terms [three menstruation periods] either take them back on equitable terms or set them free on equitable terms; But do not take them back to injure them or to take undue advantage, If anyone does that, he wrongs his own soul. Do not treat Allah's signs as a jest" (2:231).

"If any of you dies and leaves widows behind, they shall wait four months and ten days. When they have fulfilled their term, there is no blame on you if they dispose of themselves in a just manner" (2:234).

"Those of you who die and leave widows should bequeath for their widows a year's maintenance and residence. But if they [the widows] leave (the residence) there is no blame on you for what they justly do with themselves" (2:240).

13. To refuse any marriage that does not please them and more as mentioned in Quran and Ahadis.

Islam always recognised the Prominent role that women play in society. They are given the freedom to pursue any profession and they have made tremendous achievements in various fields, as so stated in earlier part of this chapter.

Rida Islam has rightly said:

In Islam, we do not need to talk about empowerment. Women are already empowered; we just need to wake up to the limitless opportunities and start implementing the position of respect that has already been conferred on us by our Creator. But this implementation requires some background work which women themselves must do. Women need to realise their true worth: We can change the world by shaping the minds of the future which is borne and nurtured in our arms. But we need to realise first that we hold such power in our hands; and then that, as is true of all real power, this task requires hard, unacknowledged years of toil.

The author further adds

Prophet Muhammad was so particular about treating children equally that once he reprimanded a person who kissed his son but not his daughter, both of them were sitting with him.

Besides, it is also mentioned:

Foeticide is a heinous crime in Islam; and female infanticide, doubly so. Allah's wrath upon those who eliminate their baby daughters is sketched so forcefully in the Quranic verse (The day) when the female child will be asked, what crime was she (punished) for.

References

1. Professor Madhu Dandavate's Besannt Lecture of Theosophical Society, Chennai on 27th December, 2001.
2. Radiance Views Weekly 30th March–5th April 2008 pp. 28-29.

2

The Concept of Marriage in Islam

Under the Muslim Law marriage is said to be both a religious rite and a contract but the nature of the contract is not that of a civil contract as defined in Section 2 of the Indian Contract Act, 1872 because of its sacramental and sacred nature. Tahir Mahmood has in his book titled 'Muslim Law in India and Abroad jointly authored with Saif Mahmood', a learned advocate of the Supreme Court of India, has also opined as under:

'Even if a Muslim marriage is a contract, it is a sacred contract– not a commercial or mercantile contract so as to attract application of the Indian Contract Act, 1872.'

Under the Muslim law, the intention of the parties is essential as also declaration and consent, when making proposal and acceptance to contract a valid marriage. Ameer Ali observes:

"Marriage is contracted by means of declaration and consent, both expressed in the preterite (tense expressing past action or state)." He further adds that under the Shiah law, however, it is not necessary that both parties should use the past tense."[1]

Hamilton's translation of the Hedaya is also to the same effect, 'Marriage is contracted, that is to say, is effected and legally confirmed by means of declaration and consent both expressed in the preterite."[2]

Baillie says: 'Marriage is contracted by declaration and acceptance when both are expressed in words of past, or when one of them is expressed in the past and the other in the imperative or the present.

Plurality of wives

The Holy Quran says:

'Marry such women as seem good to you, two, three or four; but if you fear that you cannot do justice (between them) then marry only one. (Part. IV. Ch., IV)

And the Quran further says:

"And it is not in your power to do justice between wives, even though you may covet it; but keep yourself not aloof from one with total aversion, nor leave her like one in suspense, and if you make reconciliation, and guard yourself then surely Allah is Forgiving, Merciful." (Part. V., Ch. IV)

The Quran enumerates the forbidden degrees for marriage thus.

'You are forbidden to marry your mothers and your daughters and your sisters and your paternal aunts and your maternal aunts and brother's daughters and sister's daughters and your mothers that have suckled you and the foster sisters and mothers of your wives and your stepdaughters who are in your guardianship, (born) of your wives unto whom you have visited, but if you have not visited them, there is no sin (in marrying them) and the wives of your sons who are of your own loins and that you should have two sisters together except what has already passed; for Allah is forgiving and merciful.

"And forbidden to you are all married women."

And do not marry women whom your father's married except bygones for this is abominable, sinful and an evil custom. (Part. V., Ch. IV)

The author of Taudih proceeds more logically. 'When it is admitted that marriage is prohibited, it follows that prohibition makes it void. The effect of prohibition is to create unlawfulness (hurmat) and inasmuch as marriage makes cohabitation lawful and as lawfulness itself is taken away in virtue of prohibition the contract of marriage becomes batil (void) *ab initio*. In ancient Arabia an Arab could lawfully marry two sisters and a tradition is reported by Zuahak bin Firoz.

He said, 'O Messenger of God I have become a Muslim and have two wives that are sisters.' The Prophet said, 'Choose whichever of the two you like.'

According to Deoband school of thought a Muslim can not enter into a marriage contract with persons belonging to the following categories.

1. Marriage with one's children, grand-children, great grand-children, etc. is not permissible. Nor is marriage with one's parents, grand-parents, maternal grand-parents, etc. permissible.

2. Marriage with one's brothers, uncles and nephews is not permissible. According to the Shari'ah, a brother is one whose mother and father is the same, or they have one father but two mothers, or one mother but two fathers. They are all brothers. But if the father is different, and the mother is also different; that person will not be a brother. Nikah with him will be valid.

3. Marriage with one's son-in-law is not permissible. This is irrespective of whether the daughter is already living with him or not. In all cases, *nikah* with him is *haram*.

4. A girl's father passed away. Her mother married another person. However, before the mother could even live with her new husband, she passed away or he divorced her. In such a case, the girl can marry this step-father of hers. However, if the mother lived with him, it will not be permissible for this girl to marry him.

5. *Nikah* with one's step-children is not valid. In other words, if a man has several wives, then one of the wives cannot marry the children of the co-wives. This is irrespective of whether she had lived with her husband or not. Nikah with these children is prohibited under all circumstances.

6. It is not permissible for a woman to marry her father-in-law or even the father or grand-father of her father-in-law.

7. As long as a sister is married to her husband, it is not permissible for another sister to marry this brother-in-law of hers. However, if

her sister passes away or he divorces her and she completes her iddat, it will be permissible for the other sister to marry her brother-in-law. In the case where the brother-in-law divorces the first sister, it is not permissible for the second sister to marry her brother-in-law until her sister completes her iddat.

8. If two sisters marry one person, the marriage of the sister whose *nikah* was performed first will be valid while the marriage of the sister whose *nikah* was performed later will not be valid.

9. A man married a woman. As long as he remains married to her, he cannot marry her maternal and paternal aunts and nieces.

10. If the relationship between two women is such that if we had to regard one of them as a man, their *nikah* will not be valid, then such two women cannot marry a person at the same time. When one of them passes away or one of them is divorced and completes her iddat, only then will it be permissible for the person to marry the other woman.

11. If a woman and her step-daughter marry a person at the same time, the *nikah* will be valid.

12. Adoption is not considered in the Shariah. By adopting a boy, he does not become one's son. It is therefore permissible to marry one's adopted son.

13. If a man is not one's real uncle but he becomes an uncle through some other distant relationship, marrying him is permissible. Similarly, if a man happens to be one's paternal uncle or nephew through some distant relationship, *nikah* with him is permissible. Nikah with one's cousins is also valid irrespective of whether they are paternal or maternal cousins.

14. Two women who are not blood sisters but are maternal or paternal cousins are permitted to marry one man at the same time. In the presence of such a cousin, another cousin can also marry the same man. The same rule applies to a very distant maternal or paternal aunt. That is, the niece and this distant maternal or paternal aunt can marry the same man at one time.

15. All the relations, which become haram on account of lineage also become haram on account of breast-feeding. In other words, if a

girl is breast-fed by a particular woman, then this girl cannot marry the latter's husband because he will now be regarded as her father. A girl who has been breast-fed by a particular woman cannot marry a boy who has been breast-fed by the same woman. Nor can this girl marry the children of this woman because she is also regarded as a child of this woman. All the maternal and paternal uncles and maternal and paternal nephews who become related due to this breast-feeding also become *haram* on this girl.

16. If two girls have been breast-fed by one woman, they cannot marry the same man at one time. In other words, whatever has been explained previously, will also apply to relations based on breast-feeding.

17. A man committed adultery with a certain woman. Now it will not be permissible for her mother or her children to marry this man.

18. Due to the passions of youth, a woman touched a man with evil intentions. It will now not be permissible for her mother or her children to marry this man. Similarly, if a man touches a woman with evil intentions, her mother and her children will be haram on him.

19. In the middle of the night, a man decided to awaken his wife. However, he mistakenly touched his daughter or his mother-in-law. Thinking them to be his wife, he touched them with the passions of youth. Now, this man will become haram on his wife forever. There is no way in which she can become permissible for him. It will be necessary for him to divorce his wife.

20. If a boy touches his step-mother with an evil intention, she will become *haram* on her husband. There is no way in which she can be *halal* for him. If the step-mother touches her step-son with an evil intention, the same rule will apply.

21. A Muslim woman cannot marry a man who belongs to any other religion. She can only marry a Muslim man.

22. A woman's husband divorced her or he passed away. As long as she does not complete her iddat, she cannot marry anyone else.

23. Once a woman marries a man, she cannot marry another person unless and until she is divorced by this person and also completes her iddat.

24. If a woman is not married and she falls pregnant due to adultery, it will be permissible to marry her. However, it will not be permissible to have intercourse with her until she delivers the child. But if the woman marries the same person who had committed adultery with her, it will be permissible for the person to have intercourse with her.

25. If a person has four wives, he cannot marry a fifth woman. If he happens to divorce one of his four wives, another woman cannot marry him until the one who is divorced completes her iddat.

Note: Marriages among Shias and Sunnis are not so common in India and even different Islamic scholars have different views about it.

In order for a *nikah* to be valid, it is also essential for at least two males or one male and two females to be present, to hear the *nikah* being performed, and to hear the two words (i.e. the offer and the acceptance) being uttered. Only then will the *nikah* be valid. If two persons sit together in privacy and one says to the other : "I give my daughter to you in marriage" and the other person replies : "I accept your daughter", the *nikah* will not be valid. Similarly, if the *nikah* was performed in the presence of one person only, even then the *nikah* will not be valid.

If there are no males present, but only females, the *nikah* will not be valid even if there are ten females present. Together with two females, one male has to be present.

If there are two males but they are not Muslims, the *nikah* will not be valid. Similarly, if both are Muslims but both or one of them is immature, the *nikah* will not be valid. Similarly, if there is one male and two females but both or one of the females is immature, the *nikah* will not be valid.

It is preferable to perform the *nikah* in a large gathering such as after the jumu'ah salat in a jumu'ah musjid or in any other large gathering. This is so that the *nikah* will be well announced and the people will become aware of the nikah. A *nikah* should not be performed in secret and privacy. However, if due to some reason many persons are unable to attend, then at least two males or one male and two females who hear the *nikah* being performed in their very presence should be present.

If both the man and woman are mature, they can perform their own nikah. All that they have to do is say the following in the presence of two witnesses: One of them must say: "I am making my *nikah* with you" and the other must say : "I accept." In so doing, the *nikah* will be valid.

If a person does not make his *nikah* himself, but asks someone to perform his *nikah* with someone, or, he mentions the name of the person with whom he wishes his *nikah* to be performed and this person performs this *nikah* in the presence of two witnesses - the *nikah* will be valid. Even if this person rejects or denies this later, the *nikah* will still be intact.

Who can be the WALI, that is ,the person who has the power or choice of getting a boy or girl married?

1. The first wali of a boy or girl is their father. If the father is not present, the grand-father becomes their wali. If he is not present, then the great grand-father. If none of them are present, the blood-brother becomes their wali. If he is not present, then the step-brother, i.e. brothers from one father. Thereafter, the nephew, thereafter the nephew's son; and thereafter, the nephew's grand-son. If none of them are present, the blood uncle becomes their wali. If he is not present, then the step-uncle, i.e. the step-brother of their father. Thereafter, the son of the blood uncle and thereafter his grand-son. Thereafter, the son of the step-uncle and thereafter his grand-son. If none of them are present, the father's uncle becomes their wali; and thereafter his children. If the father's uncle, his children and grand-children are not present; then the grand-father's uncle becomes their wali. Thereafter, his children, grand-children, and great grand-children.

If none of them is present, the mother will be their wali. Thereafter, the paternal grand-mother, then the maternal grand-mother and then the maternal grand-father. Thereafter, the blood-sister and then the step-sister, i.e. sisters from one father. Thereafter, the step-brother and then the step-sister who is from one mother. Thereafter, the paternal aunt, then the maternal uncle, and then the maternal aunt.

2. An immature person cannot become a wali of anyone. A non-believer cannot be a wali for any Muslim, nor can a lunatic be a wali for anyone.

3. A mature girl has the choice to marry or not to marry. She can marry whomsoever she wishes – no one can force her to marry a particular person. If she marries a person on her own, the *nikah* will be valid irrespective of whether the wali is informed or not, and irrespective of whether the wali gives his consent or not. In all cases the *nikah* will be valid. However, if she does not marry a person who is of the same social standing as her, and instead, marries a person who is of a lower standing than her family, and her wali is not happy about this marriage, then the *fatwa* in this case is that the *nikah* will not be valid.

If she marries a person who is in the same social standing as her, but the *mahr* that she receives is less then what is normally fixed in her paternal grandfather's family, then although the *nikah* will be valid, the wali will have the right to annul this marriage. The *mahr* that is normally fixed in her paternal grandfather's family is known as mahrul mithl. The wali can go to a Muslim court and have such a marriage annulled. However, it should be borne in mind that this right of annulment is only possessed by all those walis whom we had mentioned before the mother. In other words, from the father onwards till the children of the grand-father's uncle.

4. A wali performed the *nikah* of a mature girl without asking her or without seeking her consent. The validity of such a *nikah* will be dependent on her permission and consent. If she grants her permission, the *nikah* will be valid. If she does not grant her permission or is not happy, the *nikah* will not be valid. The method of granting permission is mentioned in the next mas'ala.

5. The wali came and informed a young virgin girl that he intends performing her *nikah* with a certain person, or that he has already performed her *nikah* with a certain person. Upon hearing this, she remained silent, began smiling or began to cry. All these responses of her's will be considered to be a permission and a consent. Now, if the wali performs her *nikah*, it will be valid. If he has already performed it, it will also be valid. It is not a prerequisite for her to

give a verbal permission. Those who force a girl in giving a verbal permission are in error.

6. At the time of seeking her permission, the wali did not mention the name of her future husband, nor did she have any prior knowledge of him. In such a case, her silence will not be considered to be a form of consent, nor will it be considered to be a form of granting permission. It is necessary to mention the boy's name or some other form of identification whereby the girl can understand that the wali is referring to a particular person. Similarly, if the wali performed the *nikah* without mentioning the amount of *mahr* to her and it was far less than the mahrul mithl, the *nikah* will not be valid without her permission. He will have to seek her permission again.

7. The girl is not a virgin, and instead had married previously and this is her second marriage. When the wali asks her or seeks her permission for this second marriage, her mere silence will not be considered to be a form of granting permission. Instead, she will have to give a verbal reply. If she does not give a verbal reply and remains silent, and despite this, the wali performs her nikah, then her *nikah* will be in abeyance. Later, if she gives a verbal permission, the *nikah* will be valid. If not, it will not be valid.

8. Despite the father being present, the uncle, brother or any other wali sought the permission of a virgin girl. If she remains silent, it will not be considered to be a form of granting permission. Only when she gives a verbal permission will it be considered. However, if the father sent these persons to seek her permission, her silence will be considered to be a form of consent. In short, the wali who is given the first preference in the Shari'ah and who has the most right to seek permission from the girl – when he asks her or when someone who has been sent by him asks her, then only will her silence be considered to be a form of consent. If the grand-father had the right of asking her, and instead the brother asked her; or if the brother had the right of asking her and instead she was asked by her uncle, then in such a case her silence will not be considered to be a consent.

9. A wali performed the *nikah* of a girl without asking her and without obtaining her consent. After the nikah, the wali or his messenger came and informed the girl that her *nikah* with a particular

person has been performed. In such a case, if she remains silent, this will be a permission on her part and the *nikah* will be valid. But if someone else comes and informs her, and this person is a pious, reliable person, or two persons come and inform her, then by her remaining silent the *nikah* will be valid. But if there is only one person who informs her and he is an unreliable person, then by her remaining silent the *nikah* will not be valid. Instead, it will be held in abeyance. When she gives a verbal reply or any other form of granting permission is found, then only will the *nikah* be valid.

10. Upon being informed of her nikah, the girl did not give a verbal reply although it was necessary for her to give a verbal reply. However, when her husband approached her she did not refuse him from engaging in sexual intercourse with her. Even in this case, the *nikah* will be valid.

11. The same rules apply to a mature boy, i.e. he cannot be forced into a marriage nor can the wali perform his *nikah* without his permission. If his *nikah* is performed without his permission, it's validity will be dependent on his permission. If he expresses his consent, his *nikah* will be valid. If not, it will not be valid. However, it should be borne in mind that the boy's silence is not considered to be a form of granting permission. He will have to give a verbal reply.

12. If a boy or a girl is immature, they do not have their own choice. Their *nikah* is not valid without a wali. If a boy (or girl) performs his *nikah* on his own or someone else performs it, it will be dependent on the permission of the wali. If the wali grants permission, the *nikah* will be valid. If not, it will not be valid. The wali has full rights over such a boy or girl. He can get them married to whoever he wishes and refuse whoever he wishes. Immature girls and immature boys cannot reject such a *nikah* at that time. This is irrespective of whether the girl is a virgin or had been married previously and had also been sent to her (first) husband's home - the same rule will apply.

13. If the father or grand-father perform the *nikah* of an immature girl or boy, they do not have the right to reject or repudiate this *nikah* even after they become mature. This is irrespective of whether the marriage was executed with a person who is of the same social standing or with a person of a lower class, and irrespective of whether

the *nikah* was performed with mahrul mithl or whether it was far less than the mahrul mithl. In all cases the *nikah* will be valid and they cannot reject or repudiate this nikah.

14. If a wali other than the father or grand-father performed the nikah, and it was performed with a boy of the same social standing and the mahrul mithl was also given, then in such a case the *nikah* will be valid. However, after reaching the age of maturity, she has the right to endorse this *nikah* or to go and complain to a Muslim judge and have this marriage annulled.

But if the wali performed her marriage with a person of a lower social standing or accepted a *mahr* which was far less than the mahrul mithl, the *nikah* will not be valid from the very outset. Similarly, if the wali performed the *nikah* of a boy with a *mahr* which was far more than the *mahrul mithl* of the girl, the *nikah* will not be valid from the very outset.

15. A wali other than the father or grand-father had performed the *nikah* of an immature girl who also had knowledge of this nikah. Thereafter, she became mature and until then her husband hadn't had any sexual intercourse with her. In such a case, the moment she becomes mature, she must mention her discontent with regard to marrying this person. She must clearly state that she is not happy. Alternatively, she could say that she does not wish to continue with this marriage. This could be said in the presence of others or in privacy where she is all alone. But she has to mention it verbally. However, by her merely saying this, the *nikah* will not be annulled. She will have to go to a Muslim judge, he will annul the marriage, and only then will it be annulled.

Once she becomes mature and allows even a moment to pass in which she does not mention her discontent, she will not have the choice of having her *nikah* annulled.

But if the girl did not have any knowledge of this *nikah* and only learnt of it after becoming mature, then the moment she is informed, she will immediately have the right to reject the nikah. If she remains silent for even a moment, she will forfeit this right to reject the nikah.

16. If her husband engaged in sexual intercourse with her, and thereafter she becomes mature, it is not necessary for her to reject the *nikah* immediately after becoming mature or after being informed. Instead, as long as she does not express her consent and happiness, she will have the choice of rejecting or accepting irrespective of how much time lapses. However, if she clearly states that she is happy about this marriage, or her consent is made apparent in some other way such as being in solitude with her husband like any other normal husband and wife, then she will have no choice and this *nikah* will become entrenched.

17. The person who is most entitled of being the wali of an immature girl is gone to a foreign country. He is so far away that if the rest of the family had to await his arrival in order to consult him, the girl will lose this opportunity. Furthermore, the person who has come with the proposal is not prepared to wait for so long and it will be difficult for the girl to receive a similar proposal. In such a case, the person who is next in line to become her wali can also perform her nikah. If he performs the *nikah* without consulting the girl, it will be valid. But if the first wali is not very far away, her *nikah* should not be performed without consulting him. If it is performed, it will be dependent on his permission. Once he grants his permission, the *nikah* will be valid.

18. Similarly, if the second wali performs the *nikah* of an immature girl despite the most rightful wali being present, it will be dependent on his permission. For example, if the grand-father performs the *nikah* without consulting the father despite the latter being present, it will be dependent on the father's permission. If the right belonged to the brother but the *nikah* was performed by the uncle, it will be dependent on the brother's permission.

19. A woman became a lunatic and lost her sanity. She has a mature son and a father as well. If her *nikah* has to be performed, her wali will be her son because the son is more entitled of being a wali than the father (father of the woman).

The development of the institution of marriage is a matter of historical interest. It originated in the form of irregular unions and marital unions.[3]

Polyandry, polygamy and even monogamy were enjoined by immemorial customs, and practised in different parts of the world. The transition from the sacramental indissolubility of marriage to the treatment of marriage, as a civil institution is a modern idea.[4]

The Arabian civilisation in its natural growth passed through various stages. The advent of the great Prophet of Islam marked a triumphant period, the old political and social structure of the Arabian culture tottered down, it was replaced by a refined civilisation. The Arabs themselves refer to the pre- Islamic era as the days of ignorance i.e. "period of ignorance or rather wildness or savagery, in antithesis to the moral reasonableness of a civilised man."[5]

Woman's consent is of paramount importance:

The Holy Quran emphatically denounced the custom of taking women as wives against their wishes:

Oh believers! It is not lawful for you that you should take women as heritage against their will.

The word "nikah" literally means "to unite". Subsequently, it came to be known as synonym of "marriage" or in other words, it came to denote marriage. It is said that "Nikah cannot be effected except by its pillar rukn emanating from ahl (one who is competent to contract) and in reference to mahl (fitting subject of marriage), rukn consists of proposal and acceptance and the effect hukm of it is lawfulness of enjoyment, and procreation and generation are its object." It looks like a civil contract but the fact of the matter is that this contractual relationship is a sacred bond between husband and wife. Even if it is presumed to be a civil contract for the sake of presumption, can anyone claim that the sanctity of such a contract should not be preserved?

Another view is that "Under the Muslim law"[6] marriage is both a civil contract and a religious rite. It is a devotion and act of ibadat or piety and since the earliest times (the days of Adam) it has maintained its sanctity, like faith. Muslim jurists have different views about its obligatory nature but there is a consensus of opinion that marriage is a 'Sunnat Muvakida'. 'Sunnat Muvakida' is defined as under:

" 'Sunnat Muvakida' is an institution the compliance with which is considered as virtuous and deviation from which is regarded as a sin. A person who complies with it is rewarded in the next world, and he who does not sins." **Thus, marriage is a religious rite under the Muslim law, although its nature is that of a secular transaction and a civil contract.** It is also said that the notion of contract has been introduced and brought into prominence, because it renders facility of divorce, and allows separation of parties easily in the eye of the law, whereas the sacramental aspect would make the marriage tie indissoluble.

In the celebrated book Taudih, marriage has been described as an institution which has been legalised for manifold objects, such as preservation of the species, the fixing of descent, restraining men from debauchery, the encouragement of chastity, promotion of love and union between the husband and wife, and of mutual help in earning livelihood.

Mahr (Dower or bridal money)

Mahr is the bridal money which a husband gives to his wife at the time of marriage. There is no specified rule to fix the amount of Mahr for any marriage. It depends upon financial status of the groom and is generally mutually agreed between the two parties (families of bride and groom).

The *mahr* (dowry) is something that is paid by the man to his wife. It is described as contracting to make a settlement on wife. It may be in cash or in kind. It is not something like an ordinary settlement or bargain. As a matter of fact it is paid or given to the wife as a token of respect to her indicating a serious desire to marry her with a sense of responsibility and as an assurance to perform his part of the contract.

Allah says in the Qur'an:

"And give the women their dowries with a good heart..." [Quran 4:4]:

As per Deoband school of thought, the validity of *mahr* can be adjudged in the light of the following observations:

1. Once a *nikah* is performed, it will be valid irrespective of whether mention of any *mahr* was made or not. Despite it being valid,

one will have to give the mahr. In fact, if a person makes the condition that he will not give any *mahr* and that he is marrying the woman without any mahr, he will still have to give the mahr.

2. The minimum *mahr* is 10 dirhams and there is no limit to the maximum amount of mahr. The woman can stipulate as much as she wishes. However, it is not good to stipulate a very high figure. If a person gives an amount less than 10 dirhams or its equivalent, he will have to give the balance as well because *mahr* cannot be an amount less than the minimum. If the husband divorces his wife (in this case) even before she can come and live with him, he will have to give half of the minimum.

3. A person stipulated R20, R100, R1000, or any other amount according to his financial position. The woman thereafter came and lived with him. He also had sexual intercourse with this wife of his. Alternately, he did not have intercourse with her, but he and his wife were able to meet in privacy where no one or nothing stopped them or prevented them from engaging in sexual intercourse. In both these cases, it will be wajib on the person to fulfil the full amount of the stipulated mahr. If none of the above transpired between them, and one of them passed away, it will still be wajib to fulfil the entire mahr. Furthermore, if none of the above transpired between them, and the man divorced her, it will be wajib on him to fulfil half the stipulated mahr.

In short, if the husband and wife meet in privacy, as mentioned above or one of them passes away, the entire *mahr* becomes wajib. And if the husband divorces her prior to them being in privacy and seclusion, it will be wajib to fulfil half the stipulated mahr.

4. If one of them was ill, keeping a fast of Ramadan, in the ihram of hajj, the woman was in her hayd or there was someone who was peeping at them or intruding on their privacy, and they met in private or seclusion in any of the above situations, then this privacy or seclusion of their's is not considered. If they meet each other in any of the above situations or circumstances, the total amount of *mahr* will not become wajib. If the husband divorces her, it will be her right to receive half the total mahr. However, if the fast was not a fast of Ramadan, instead it was a qada, nadhr, or nafl fast, and this was

being kept by one of them, then in such a case if they happened to meet in privacy and seclusion, the wife will have the right of receiving the full amount of the mahr. It will be wajib on the husband to fulfill the full amount.

5. The husband is impotent, however, both of them met in privacy and seclusion. The wife will still receive the full mahr. Similarly, if the husband is a hermaphrodite and they meet in privacy and seclusion and thereafter he divorces her, she will receive the full mahr.

6. The husband and wife met in privacy and seclusion but the wife is so young that she is incapable of sexual intercourse. Alternately, the husband is so young that he is incapable of sexual intercourse. If they meet in privacy and seclusion in such a case, the full *mahr* will not be wajib.

7. If no mention whatsoever of the *mahr* was made at the time of the nikah, or the *nikah* was performed on the condition that the woman will not receive any mahr, and thereafter one of them passed away or they met in privacy – that is regarded as a valid privacy in the Shar i 'ah - even then the *mahr* will have to be fulfilled. However, in such a case, the mahrul mithl will have to be paid.

In the above case, if the husband divorced his wife prior to being in seclusion with her, she will have no right to receive any mahr. Instead, she will only receive a set of clothing. It is wajib on the man to give this to the woman. He will be sinning if he does not do so.

8. When giving this set of clothing, only four items are wajib on the man: a dress, a scarf, a pant, and a sheet, which can cover her body from head to toe. Apart from these items, it is not wajib to give any other clothing.

9. The clothing that the man gives should be according to his financial position. If the man is poor, he should give cotton clothing. If he is of a middle class, he should give silk that is of an inferior quality. If he is very rich, he should give silk clothing that is of a very high quality. However, it should be borne in mind that in all these circumstances the clothing that is given should not be more than half the mahrul mithl in value. At the same time, it should not be less than five dirhams in value.

In other words, it is not wajib on the man to give clothing which is very expensive and which exceeds half the mahrul mithl in value. However, it is permissible for him to give clothing that is more than the stipulated amount provided that he gives it happily and out of his own will.

10. At the time of the *nikah* no *mahr* was stipulated. However, after the nikah, the husband and wife agreed upon a specific amount as mahr. In such a case, mahrul mithl will not have to be given. Instead, the amount that they had agreed upon will have to be given. But if the husband divorced his wife prior to their meeting in privacy and seclusion, she will not have any right of receiving any mahr. Instead, she will only receive the clothing that had been mentioned previously.

11. A person stipulated R100, R1000 or any other amount according to his financial position. Thereafter the husband decided to give more than the original amount that was stipulated. This he did voluntarily and out of his own good will. For example, the stipulated *mahr* was R100, but he decided to give R150. Whatever additional amount he decides to give will now become wajib upon him. If he does not give it, he will be sinning. But if he divorces her prior to meeting in privacy and seclusion, he will have to give half of the original amount that was stipulated. The additional amount that he had decided to give will not be calculated.

Similarly, if the wife happily and willingly reduces the amount of mahr, it will be considered to be reduced. If she absolves him from paying the entire amount, it will be absolved. Now she has no right to claim it.

12. If the husband pressurised her into reducing the *mahr* or instilled some fear into her so that she reduces the mahr, then by her reducing or forgiving her husband, it will not be considered to be forgiven. It will still be wajib upon him to fulfil the mahr.

13. No cash, gold or silver was stipulated for the mahr. Instead, a small village, a farm or some land was stipulated. This is permissible. The farm, land, etc. that was stipulated will have to be given.

14. A horse, elephant or any other animal was stipulated as mahr. However, a specific horse or a specific elephant was not stipulated.

This is also permissible. In such a case an average horse which is not too cheap nor too expensive will have to be given. Alternatively, it's value in cash could be given. However, if an animal was stipulated without specifying the type of animal, this will not be valid. Mahrul mithl will have to be given.

15. A couple got married in an unlawful way and the husband and wife were therefore made to separate. For example, they got married in secret without the presence of two witnesses. Alternately, two witnesses were present but they were deaf and were therefore unable to hear the words that make a *nikah* valid. Alternatively, a man had divorced his wife or he had passed away. Prior to completing her *iddat*, the woman married another man. Or some other form of unlawful marriage had taken place and the husband and wife were therefore made to separate. However, in all these cases, the man did not have any sexual intercourse with this woman. In such a case, she will not receive any mahr. In fact, even if they met in privacy and seclusion, she will still not be eligible to receive any mahr. But if sexual intercourse had taken place, she will receive mahrul mithl. However, if at the time of *nikah* some *mahr* had been stipulated and this *mahr* is less than the mahrul mithl, then she will receive the *mahr* that had been stipulated at the time of the *nikah* and not the mahrul mithl.

16. A person had sexual intercourse with a woman after mistaking her for his wife. He will have to give her mahrul mithl as well, and this intercourse with her will not be regarded as adultery (zina) nor will there be any sin. In fact, if the woman falls pregnant, the lineage of the child will be in order. It will not be tainted and it is not permissible to label the child as being illegitimate. The moment the man realises that this is not his wife, he should immediately separate himself from her and it will not be permissible for him to continue with the intercourse. It is also wajib on this woman to observe the *iddat*. It is not permissible for her to stay with her husband or to engage in sexual intercourse with him. The rules related to *iddat* will be mentioned in a later chapter - Insha'Allah.

17. If in a certain place or country, the norm is that the entire *mahr* must be given on the first night, then the woman has the right

to demand the *mahr* on the first night. If she does not ask for it on the first night, she can ask for it whenever she wishes and it will be wajib on the husband to give it to her. He cannot delay in fulfilling the *mahr*.

18. The practice in India is that the paying and receiving of *mahr* is undertaken after divorce or after death. When the woman is divorced, it is only then that she claims her mahr. Alternatively, when the husband dies and leaves behind some wealth, she takes her *mahr* from this left over wealth of his. If the woman dies, her inheritors claim the mahr. As long as the husband and wife are living together, no one pays the *mahr* nor does she ask for it. In such a situation, the woman cannot demand the *mahr* before divorce. However, it is wajib on the man to give an amount that is normally given in that place on the first night. But if all these practices are not found in any place, these rules will not apply.

19. If the husband does not give the amount of *mahr* that is normally given before hand, the wife has the right to refuse him to engage in sexual intercourse with her until he pays that amount. If they engaged in intercourse once, she still has the right of refusing him the next time or the following time if he does not pay the mahr. If he wishes to take her to another city or country, she has the right of not going unless her *mahr* is paid. Similarly, if the *mahr* is not paid and the woman wishes to travel to another city or country, or wishes to go to her parents home, and there is a mahram who can take her, then the husband does not have the right to stop her. But once he pays the mahr, she does not have the right to do any of these things without her husband's permission. It is not permissible for her to go anywhere without his consent. As for the husband, he can take her wherever he wishes. It is not permissible for her to refuse him.

20. The husband gave some item (or cash, gold, silver, etc.) to his wife with the intention that it is mahr. Whatever he gives will be regarded as part of the mahr. It is not necessary for him to inform his wife at the time of giving it to her that he is giving her mahr.

21. The man gave an item to his wife. She claims that the item was given as a gift and not as *mahr* while the man claims that he gave it as mahr. In this case, the husband's claim will be considered.

However, if the item was such that it is consumed as food or drink, it will not be considered to be *mahr* and the husband's claim will not be considered.

Mahrul Mithl

1. Family *mahr* or mahrul mithl is determined in the following way: look at any woman in the girl's father's family who is similar or equal to this girl. That is, if the girl is young, the woman must also be young at the time of marriage. If the woman is beautiful, this girl must also be beautiful. If the woman's marriage had taken place when she was a virgin, this girl's marriage must also take place while she is a virgin. The wealth that this girl possesses at the time of her nikah, that woman also had possessed the same at the time of her nikah. The place or locality from which this girl is, that woman must also be from the same place. If this girl is religious-minded, intelligent, well-mannered and educated, that woman must also be the same. In short, this girl whose *nikah* is being performed now, must also possess the qualities that woman possessed at the time of her nikah,. If they share the same qualities, then the *mahr* that was stipulated for that woman will be the mahrul mithl for this girl.

2. Women of the girl's father's family refer to the girl's sisters, paternal aunts, cousins (children of paternal uncles), etc. In other words, girls or women who are connected to her paternal grandmother, when determining the mahrul mithl, the *mahr* of the mother is not considered. However, if her mother is also of the same family as that of her father's, e.g. if her father marries his cousin (paternal uncle's daughter), then the mother's *mahr* will also be regarded as mahrul mithl.

Age for marriage under the Muslim Law

As per Shariah, a girl having attained puberty could marry without consent of her parents and enter into contract of marriage. Puberty is the functional capability of procreation; potency to bear or beget children. However, several Muslim/Non-Muslim countries have prescribed minimum age for marriage and now the rule of puberty is an exception and not a rule even in some theocratic states. In India, too, we have such a law. It is titled as 'Child Marriage Restraint Act.'

Africa

Country	Male	Female
Algeria	19	19
(Lower with judicial permission if otherwise justified.)		
Egypt	18	18
(The age was raised in 2008 from 16 to 18 for females.)		
Libya	20	20
(Lower with judicial permission if otherwise justified with guardian's agreement.)		
Morocco	18	18
(Law not strictly followed in rural areas. Some of the judges do not uphold this law and let women younger than 18 marry.)		
Nigeria	18	18 (similar pattern not followed in different States)
Senegal	20	16
Somalia	18	18
(Court may grant exemption from minimum age, if otherwise justified.)		
South Africa	18	15
Sudan	Puberty	
(With requirement for consent of both parties.)		
South Sudan	18	
(With the consent of both parties, under the South Sudan Child Act 2008.)		
Tanzania	18	15
(The Penal Code provides that persons of "African or Asiatic descent" may marry or permit marriage of a girl under 12 in accordance with their custom or religion if marriage is not intended to be consummated before she is 12.)		
Tunisia	20	17

Country	*Male*	*Female*
(Lower with judicial special permission with a clear interest for both spouses for pressing reasons.)		
Zimbabwe	18	16
Asia		
Afghanistan	18	16
(In some cases, even younger girls are married.)		
Azerbaijan	18	17
Bangladesh	21	18
(Bangladeshi law provides for penal sanctions for under-age marriages but such marriages are not considered invalid.)		
Brunei	No minimum marriage age specified	
People's Republic of China	22	20
Hong Kong	21	(16 with parental consent.)
India	21	18
(In 2012, Delhi High Court has declared that Muslim women can marry at 15. The Law Commission report also declares that "In spite of these legal provisions, child marriage is still widely practiced and a marriage solemnised in contravention of these provisions is not void even under the new PCMA, 1929, the "Hindu Marriage Act, 1955 and also under the Muslim Law.")		
Indonesia	19	16
(Marriage at younger age is legal with parental consent and judicial approval.)		
Iran	18	15
Iraq	18	18
Japan	20	18
Jordan	18	18
(Court permission is required for females under 18 to marry men older by 20 years or more.)		
Kazakhstan	18	16
Kuwait	18	15
Lebanon	18	17

Country	*Male*	*Female*
(15, or 9 with judicial permission for Shias. 18 or 17 and 16 or 15 with judicial permission for Druze.)		
Malaysia	21	18
(Muslim girls under 16 can marry with the permission of sharia authorities.)		
Maldives	15	
(According to custom, the minimum age for marriage is 15. The Law on the Protection of the Rights of the Child discourages marriage before the age of 16.)		
Nepal	21	18
(18 for males and 16 for females with parental permission.)		
Pakistan	18	16
Palestinian territories	16	15
(As per Lunar calendar)		
Philippines	18 (15 for Muslim Males & Females)	
(If any spouse is 18–20 years and the consent of "parental" authority is not met, marriage may be prevented or annulled by any party that demands it. On the other hand, Muslim marriages in the Philippines are based on the sharia: 15 years for males and as for females, the onset of puberty to age 15, whichever comes first.)		
Russia	18	
(16 in special circumstances varying in different regions.)		
Saudi Arabia At present 'none'		
Singapore	21	18
Sri Lanka	18	
(However, the parties must have a Quazi's permission to marry before contracting into marriage if they are Muslims.)		
Syria	18	17
(Judicial discretion for males of 15 and females of 13; judge may withhold permission for marriage if court finds incompatibility in age between betrothed parties.)		

Country	*Male*	*Female*
Republic of China (Taiwan)		20
(18 for males, and 16 for females with parental consent.)		
Thailand	17	
(In certain circumstances earlier with judicial permission.)		
Turkey	18	17 with parental consent, 16 in special circumstances with court approval.
Uzbekistan	18	17 17 and 16 correspondingly in special conditions.
Vietnam	20	18
Yemen	Nonc	
(In practice, Yemeni law allows girls of any age to wed, but it forbids sex with them until the indefinite time they are 'suitable for sexual intercourse')		
Europe		
Albania	18	
Armenia	18	17
Austria	18	
(16 with parental consent but the other partner must be 18 or older.)		
Belarus	18	
Belgium	18	
(Younger with parental and judicial consent, but permission is only granted in "extreme" situations such as pregnancy.)		
Bulgaria	18	
(16 with parental consent and permission of the local court but the other partner must be 18 or older.)		
Croatia	18	(16 with court permission.)
Cyprus	18	
Czech Republic	18	

Country	***Male***	***Female***

(16 with parental consent but the other partner must be 18 or older.)

Denmark 18

(15 with an exemption named "Kongebrev" which is a letter from the king granting an exemption.)

Estonia 18 (15 with parental or court consent.)

Finland 18

(Under 18 with the consent of the Ministry of Justice in extraordinary circumstances, in which case parents or other guardian must be heard, but actual parental consent is not required.)

France 18

(But the age condition may be waived with a special dispense granted by the authorities if at least one parent consents to the marriage (or one grandparent if both parents are dead or unable to give consent, or a family council if all parents and grandparents are dead or unable to give consent). Georgia 18 (15 with parental consent.)

Germany 18

(16 with court permission and parental consent.)

Gibraltar 18

Greece 18

(16 with consent from both parents and court permission.)

Hungary 18 (16 with parental consent.)

Iceland 18

(Under 18 with parental consent and permission of the Ministry of the Interior.)

Ireland 18 (Under 18 with the court's permission.)

Italy 18 (16 with court consent.)

Latvia 18

(16 with court and/or parental permission.)

Lithuania 18

Country	*Male*	*Female*
(15 with court permission, minors can only marry below 15 if they are pregnant females with court permission.)		
Netherlands	18	
(Under 18 with parental consent; in case of pregnancy or with personal permission from the Minister of Justice.)		
Norway	18	
[16 with consent from parents (guardian) and permission from the County Governor.]		
Malta	18	(17 with parental consent.)
Poland	18	(16 for women with judicial approval.)
Portugal	18	
(16 with parental consent or if this is unattainable, the court can provide the consent).		
Romania	18	
(16 with permission from the district's administrative board.)		
Russia	18	
(16 in special circumstances, but different rules apply in some regions.)		
Serbia	18	(16 with court consent.)
Slovakia	18	
(16 with court consent, with a serious reason such as pregnancy.)		
Slovenia	18	15 with parental consent.
Spain	18	(16 with parental consent.)
Sweden	18	
(Under 18 with permission from the County Administrative Board.)		
Switzerland	18	
Turkey	18	

Country	*Male*	*Female*

(17 with parental consent, 16 in special circumstances with court approval.)

Ukraine 18

United Kingdom

England and Wales 18 (16 with parental consent.)

Scotland 16

Northern Ireland 18

(16 with parental consent (with the court able to give consent in some cases.)

Vatican City 18

(16 for males and 14 for females with parental or judicial consent per code of canon law.)

North America

Canada 18

(Varies by province, but generally 18 years old, 16 years with parental consent, and 15 years with judicial consent.)

Mexico 18 (16 for males, 15 for females.)

Puerto Rico 21

(Younger parties may obtain license in case of pregnancy or birth of child, and 18 with parental consent.)

United States 18

(Varies by state, but generally 18, with two exceptions: 19 in Nebraska and 21 in Mississippi. Most states, however, allow minors below 18 to marry (generally they have to be at least 16 but sometimes lower) with parental and/or judicial consent. Some states allow female minors below 18 to marry without parental or judicial consent, if she is pregnant.)

Brazil 18

(16 with parental or guardian consent. The marriage of someone who is under 16 years can also be authorised, but only in cases of

Country	Male	Female

pregnancy, or to avoid the imposition of a criminal penalty (statutory rape).

Country	Male	Female
Bolivia	16	14
Chile	18	(16 with parental consent.)
Colombia	18	(15 with parental consent.)
Ecuador	18	
Paraguay	16	14
Peru	18	
Venezuela	18	

(15 for females and 16 for males with parental consent)

Sometimes, it is propagated that the child marriage is common in Muslim countries but the figures quoted above reveal that it is not peculiar to Muslim states as most of the countries alow persons below the age of 18, 17 and 16 years to marry, of course, subject to certain riders.

References

1. *Mahemmedan law* Vol. II, p. 329.
2. Hedaya (Grady) Bk. II, p. 25.
3. 'Marital unions are the outcome of sexual selection and restrictions' Vinogradoff Historical Jurisprudence Vol.1., p. 167.
4. 'In civil society it becomes a civil contract regulated and prescribed by law' Story conflict of laws p. 143.
5. Nicholson's 'Literary History of the Arabs' p. 30.
6. 'Muhammadan Jurisprudence purports to be in fact a science of man's rights and duties both spiritual and social, Abdur Rahim, Jurisprudence, p. VII.

3

The Concept of Divorce in Islam

Talak (Talaque) in its literal sense is "the taking off any tie or restrain", and in law it signifies a dissolution of a marriage.

Under Muslim law divorce appears to be an arbitrary act of a husband as if he may divorce his wife at his pleasure with or without her consent and without any cogent reason(s). But a true and devout Muslim is not supposed to act arbitrarily. He should regulate his life according to the tenets of Islam and should not take any decision arbitrarily and capriciously. Divorce is condemned by Islam in unequivocal terms.

The Muslim Law concedes the right of repudiation; but prohibits the exercise of this arbitrary power by threats of divine displeasure.[1]

The Holy Quran not only discourages divorce; but suggests procedure for the reconciliation of the married parties under divine blessings.

"If you fear enmity between the
husband and wife, then appoint a referee
from his people and a referee from her
people. If they both desire a reconciliation,
Allah will effect harmony
between them. Surely Allah is knowing and aware."

(Part. V, Ch. IV)

Thus, divorce is condemned and discouraged by Islam and such an option should be exercised only when it becomes imperative or inevitable. In other words Quran sanctioned divorce as a legitimate mode of separation or dissolution of marriage only in extreme cases of unhappiness, disharmony and misery when there is no way out.

The Prophet (Prophet Muhammad) commanded:

God has not created anything upon the face of this earth which He dislikes more than divorce.

In 'Story's Conflict of Laws' Lord Robertson's following observation at page 144 also deserves serious consideration:

"The contract of marriage is the most important of all human transactions. It is the very basis of the whole fabric of civilised society. The status of marriage is *juris gentium*, and the foundation of it, like that, of all other contracts, rests on the consent of the parties. But it differs from other contracts, in this, that the rights, obligations, or duties arising from it are not left entirely to be regulated by agreements of parties, but are, to a certain extent, matters of municipal regulation over which the parties have no control by any declaration of their will......Unlike other contracts, it cannot, in general, amongst civilised nations, be dissolved by mutual consent, and it subsists in full force although one of the parties should be forever rendered incapable, as in the case of incurable insanity or the like, from performing his part of the contract."

As stated earlier, marriage is regarded by all the jurists, as Sunnat Muvakida. Sunnat Muvakida is defined as under:

"Sunnat Muvakida' is an institution the compliance with which is considered as virtuous and deviation from which is regarded as a sin. A person who complies with it is rewarded in the next world, and he who does not sins." Hence, marriage is a religious rite under the Muslim law, although it is in the form of a secular transaction and a civil contract. The notion of contract is brought into prominence, because it renders facility of divorce, and allows separation of parties easily in the eye of the law, whereas the sacramental aspect would make the marriage tie indissoluble.

In the celebrated book Taudih, marriage is described as an institution which has been legalised for manifold objects, such as preservation of the species, the fixing of descent, restraining men from debauchery, the encouragement of chastity, promotion of love and union between the husband and wife, and of mutual help in earning livelihood. Islam provides ample provisions for the repudiation and cancellation of marriage. It grants to the husband the supreme power of divorce at will; but it allows the wife to contract at the time of the marriage, or thereafter to delegate the power of divorce to a third person, or reserve it to herself. This is technically known as the doctrine of Tafveez-ul-Tulak; while other forms of repudiations effected by mutual agreement and on payment of compensation are known, as "mubarat" and "khula" respectively. The abuse or recklessness with which the right of divorce may be exercised by the husband is restricted by threats of divine displeasure.

AL-HAJ MAHOMED ULLAH Ibn S. JUNG, has, in the concluding paragraph of his book titled 'The Muslim Law of Marriage' (Compiled from the original Arabic authorities) stated as under:

'Under the Muslim Law divorce is an arbitrary act of a husband and he may divorce his wife at his pleasure with or without her consent. Divorce may be verbal only and no special expressions are necessary; it suffices, if it denotes a clear intention to dissolve the marriage, and writing is not necessary to the legal validity of divorce. Divorce is either revocable or irrevocable. During the period of iddat, the husband may take back his wife, but after the period has elapsed he cannot exercise this right; marriage is deemed to subsist with respect to various of its effects such as maintenance, residence and right of inheritance. The husband can delegate to a third person or to his wife the power to repudiate herself. Khula is a repudiation by consent and is at the instance of the wife for a valuable consideration Mubarat is a divorce by mutual consent. Judicial separations are technically known as Tafrik, they take place for, various causes. Divorce during death-illness, marz-ul-maut is ineffective. Divorce does not affect a woman whose marriage is batil (void) *ab initio*. The dissolution of such a marriage is by separation. However, divorce is condemned by Islam and it should not be resorted to, unless it has become imperative and absolutely necessary.'

India is not a theocratic state and all Indians are governed by the law made by the legislatures—the parliament or state legislatures. In India, decree for dissolution of marriage, can be obtained under the Dissolution of Muslim Marriages Act, 1939[2] and the entire procedure is regulated by this Act. Section 2 of the Act deals with the grounds for decree for dissolution of marriage as under:

A woman married under Muslim law shall be entitled to obtain a decree for the dissolution of her marriage on any one or more of the following grounds, namely:

(i) that the whereabouts of the husband have not been known for a period of four years;

(ii) that the husband has neglected or has failed to provide for her maintenance for a period of two years;

(iii) that the husband has been sentenced to imprisonment for a period of seven years or upwards;

(iv) that the husband has failed to perform, without reasonable cause, his marital obligations for a period of three years;

(v) that the husband was impotent at the time of the marriage and continues to be so;

(vi) that the husband has been insane for a period of two years or is suffering from leprosy or a virulent venereal disease;

(vii) that she, having been given in marriage by her father or other guardian before she attained the age of fifteen years, repudiated the marriage before attaining the age of eighteen years:

Provided that the marriage has not been consummated;

(viii) that the husband treats her with cruelty, that is to say,—

(a) habitually assaults her or makes her life miserable by cruelty of conduct even if such conduct does not amount to physical ill-treatment, or

(b) associates with women of evil repute or leads an infamous life, or

(c) attempts to force her to lead an immoral life, or

(d) disposes of her property or prevents her exercising her legal rights over it, or

(e) obstructs her in the observance of her religious profession or practice, or (f) if he has more wives than one, does not treat her equitably in accordance with the injunctions of the Quran;

(ix) on any other ground which is recognised as valid for the dissolution of marriages under Muslim law:

Provided that—

(a) no decree shall be passed on ground (iii) until the sentence has become final;

(b) a decree passed on ground (i) shall not take effect for a period of six months from the date of such decree, and if the husband appears either in person or through an authorised agent within that period and satisfied the Court that he is prepared to perform his conjugal duties, the Court shall set aside the said decree; and

(c) before passing a decree on ground (v) the Court shall, on application by the husband, make an order requiring the husband to satisfy the Court within a period of one year from the date of such order that he has ceased to be impotent, and if the husband so satisfies the Court within such period, no decree shall be passed on the said ground.

Besides, The Muslim Personal Law (Shariat) Application Act, 1937[3] was also enacted to make provision for the application of the Muslim Personal Law (Shariat) to Muslims. Section 2 of the Act provides as under:

Application of personal law to Muslims.—Notwithstanding any customs or usage to the contrary, in all questions (save questions relating to agricultural land) regarding intestate succession, special property of females, including personal property inherited or obtained under contract or gift or any other provision of Personal Law, marriage, dissolution of marriage, including talaq, ila, zihar, lian, khula and mubaraat, maintenance, dower, guardianship, gifts, trusts and trust properties, and wakfs (other than charities and charitable institutions and charitable and religious endowments) the rule of decision in cases where the parties are Muslims shall be the Muslim Personal Law (Shariat) Act,1937.

References

1. Baillie's Digest p. 205, "but has been permitted for the avoidance of greater evils."
2. The Dissolution of Muslim Marriages Act, 1939.
3. The Muslim Personal Law (Shariat) Application Act, 1937.

4

Status of Widow in Islam

It is no taboo to be a widow in Islam. She is as good as any other woman in the society. Second marriage of a widow is permissible in Islam. Status of widow can be assessed and determined in the light of the personal life of Prophet Mohammad. The Prophet himself married his first wife Khadija, who was a widow and thereafter Umme Salmah, also a widow.

It is said that widow marriages were uncommon in ancient Arabia; but this seems very unlikely, as the custom of sons and heirs inheriting their relative's and father's widows was prevalent; the fact that the ancient Arabs, did not allow widows to marry whomsoever they liked, is consistent with the traditional belief that a woman was not a free agent in marriage. It was the right of her father, brother, cousin or relation to give her hand in marriage. The sons and relatives did not permit widows to marry outside their family.

Muslims are commanded to honour, respect and be kind and charitable towards widows. They are required to treat them nicely. Islam forbids the mistreatment of widows. It thus reformed centuries old Arabian culture that valued virgin brides but had a poor record of taking care of widows and their children. The issue of widows was particularly important for the Muslims because many a Muslim woman had lost their husbands during war in Mecca.

Special Status

Islam grants special status to widows and other vulnerable groups, such as, orphans, the poor and female infants. In Islam, taking care of widows is considered a charitable act of a very high order. According to Book 73, Number 36, of the Sahih Bukhari, the Prophet once said: "The one who looks after and works for a widow and for a poor person is like a warrior fighting for Allah's cause."

The Quran, too, is filled with commands to take care of the orphans and the widows. The Quran, in surah 4, verse 19, also explicitly forbids a common abuse in Prophet's time: forcing her to marry someone or do other things against her will.

The hadith of Sahih Bukhari, Book 38, Number 504, relates a story that bears testimony to Prophet Muhammad's positive attitude towards widows. A man, named, Jabir bin Abdullah was selling a camel to the Prophet. At that time it was brought to light that Abdullah had married a widow. The Prophet asked him as to why he had not married a virgin. Thereupon, he replied that he preferred a matured woman to take care of his children. The Prophet appreciated his action and ordered that Abdullah be paid extra money in addition to the price of the camel for his wisdom and charitable act.

Muslim widows are at liberty to re-marry. The only condition on widows is the waiting period between their husbands' death and remarriage. According to surah 2, verse 234, of the Quran, a widow must wait four lunar months and 10 days after her husband's death before re-marrying. Once this period of mourning is over, they are free to choose husbands and the potential husbands may make offers to them.

5

Interpretation of the Holy Quran, Ahadis[1] and Ancient Texts

In the present legal scenario and in the modern jurisprudential terminology, the Quran may well be described as the final legislative Code of Islam. It is the '*Fons publici privatique iuris*', and '*Finis aequi iuris*' of the science of Muslim jurisprudence, or it may well be described in the language of Livy as "*Corpus omnis Muslim iuris*".

The Law of Islam is mainly based on the Quran and the Ahadis (traditions) of the Holy Prophet. The Quran is the divine communication and revelation to the Prophet of Islam. These communications are by way of commands governing the private or public, religious and secular rights and duties of the Muslims of the world.

The Quran boldly enunciates:

"Say if mankind and ginni should combine together to bring out the like of this Quran, they will not bring the like of it, even though some of them helped the others." (Part XV, Ch. XVII)

According to Sir William Muir, as so stated in his book titled "The life of Mahomed", at page 563, the characteristic of the Muslim law is the complete identification of its origin with personality of the Prophet of Islam.

Ahadis (traditions) consist of the actions, precepts and teachings of the Prophet and their authenticity rests on the "Sunnat." For long they were circulated orally and in course of time some private collections were compiled. During the reign of the Omayad Khalif Omar II, Imam Malik prepared a famous collection known as the "Muwatta." Imam Bukhari collected 600,000 traditions and after a careful selection he included about 8,000 in his famous book "The Kitab-ul-Jami-us Sahih." This celebrated collection was followed by the juristic works of the five great traditionists Muslim, Abu Daud, Tirmizi, Nasai and Ibn Maja. All these are known as "Al-Kutubus Sitta", and are universally revered by the Muslim world. The traditions are divided into four principal divisions. "Hadisul Mutwatir, Sahih, Hasan and Zaif", the essential test is that it should not be contrary to the Quran.

The influence of these traditionists on jurisprudence was great as it served to bridge up the differences between the four great schools and helped in resolving various disputes between different parties.

When a question as to the interpretation to be put on a text of the Quran arises it is the duty of the courts to see how the text has been interpreted by the Muslim jurists of recognised merit and authority and their own exposition would be treated as authoritative. The Courts should not attempt to put their own construction on the Quran in opposition to the express rulings of Muhammadan commentators of great antiquity and high authority.[2]

It is quite improper for the Courts to speculate on the mode in which the particular text can be reconciled with the law as laid down in the work of some great authorities (e.g. the Hedaya).[3]

If a rule is well settled in the view of the ancient expositors it cannot be rejected on the ground that it appears to be illegal and unsound, provided of course, that it is not contrary to equity, justice and good conscience.[4] The judges have to administer without in any way circumventing for deviating from the original text the law as promulgated by the Islamic law-givers to suit the present day conditions; and in doing so it has to be remembered that Courts are not at liberty to refuse to administer any portion of those tenets even though in certain respects they may not sound quite modern.[5]

The Quran is a divine book, that is, the Book of Allah (Almighty God), the Wise and Worthy of all Praise, Who has promised to safeguard it from any violations in its purity. It becomes incumbent upon each and every Muslim to regulate his life according to it, to implement its commandments and to pay homage to the magnificence of the One Who revealed it. Thus, Quran is a unique book with Supreme Author (Almighty God), and eternal message, universal relevance and a Complete code of Conduct covering every area of life—spiritual, intellectual, cultural, social, Political, or economic. Since The Quran is a divine book a clear injunction in it is binding and no departure or deviation is permissible provided that if the effective cause of injunction has disappeared or it is found that the injunction was in respect of a particular case and its further extension is not warranted or there is no cogent ground justifying its prospective application.

The Quran was revealed more than 1400 years ago, but its interpretation as also the interpretation of ancient texts even according to the latest rules of interpretation propounded by persons like Maxwell etc. and as interpreted by the Supreme Court of India and Courts of other countries may yield positive results. Dr Abdur-Rahim has dealt with some rules of interpretation of Quran in his book Principles of Mohammedan Jurisprudence at pages 77 to 112. Some of these rules, not being inconsistent with modern rules of interpretation are briefly stated as under:

(a) It is the duty of the interpreter to know the intention of the law giver or the expounder of the law. What has been left unexpressed or what is implied, necessary inference may be drawn from the surrounding circumstances to ascertain the intention of the law given and to arrive at the correct conclusion. For example, if the law giver fully knowing that certain customs are prevalent in the society and the law giver does not promulgate any laws prohibiting them it will be presumed that such customs have sanction of the authority in command. Likewise, if a companion of the Prophet narrates a tradition it will be presumed that he considered it to be genuine.

(b) If there are two conflicting and contradictory general speeches on sanctioning and action and the other prohibiting one the latter shall prevail.

(c) When a general proposition is qualified by a dependent Clause, then, so far as it is not so qualified it retains its characteristics as a legal authority.

(d) Statement made in answer to an inquiry or in respect of a particular occurrence, according to the general rule as accepted by consensus of opinion among the learned will be taken into account as the generality of expression use in a proposition and not the particularity of the cause that led to it.

(e) If there are two propositions, one being absolute and the other qualified what is laid down by one is distinct from the other effect should be given to both of them.

(f) The meaning of a word must be clear, manifest, explicit, unequivocal or fixed or obscure, difficult, vague or unintelligible and as such meaning of a word should be discovered with reference to its nature.

(g) Words should be interpreted in the ordinary sense unless the context requires otherwise.

(h) If a word is used in its dictionary sense it should be taken as such and if it is used in some other sense, such as, legal, conventional or technical their application should be made with reference to the sense of the word in which it should be used.

(i) When two texts are genuinely in conflict with each other the earlier one shall be repealed by the latter one as it can and should not be conceived that two inconsistent texts should remain in force at a time.

As regards authenticity and interpretation of Ahadis and ancient texts, a quotation from Al-Risala, reproduced below, and cited to in Mst. Khurshid Jan V. Fazal Dad, 1964 P.L.D. (WP.) Lah, 558 at pp. 590, 598, has a direct bearing on it.

"The Sunna which the Holy Prophet has laid down on matter for which a text is to be found in the book of God is always in full agreement with that text and clarifying on God's behalf a general text the Holy Prophet's specification is more explicit than the text.

But as for the Sunna which he laid down on matters for which a text is not founded in the Quran, the obligation to accept them rests upon us by virtue of the duty imposed by God to obey the Prophet's orders. As to the abrogating and abrogated Sunnas like the abrogating communications laid down by God to abrogate orders they are in like manner laid down by the Holy Prophet so that each Sunna may be abrogated by another. As to the contradictory traditions where no indications exist to specify which is the abrogating and the abrogated, they are all in accord with one another and contradiction does not really exist among them. For the Holy Prophet being an Arab by tongue and by country may have laid down as general rule intended to be general and another general rule intended to be particular, or a certain question may had been asked to which he gave certain concise answer, leading some of the transmitters to relate the tradition in detail and others in brief, rendering the meaning of the tradition partly clear and partly vague, or it may happen that the transmitter of a certain tradition related the answer he heard from the Holy Prophet without knowing what the question had been for had he known the question he would have understood the answer clearly from the reasoning on which the answer was based. The Holy Prophet may have likewise laid down a Sunna covering a particular situation and another covering different one, but some of those who related that they heard failed to distinguish between the two differing situations for which he has laid down the Sunnas. And he may have laid down a Sunna on a certain matter in conformity with the text of the Quran—transmitted by one authority and another in one form in another contradictory to it owing to changes in the circumstance—transmitted by another authority. Hence, the transmission by one authority appeared to many as contradictory to the other, while in reality no contradiction existed at all. He may have also provided a Sunna consisting of an order of permission or prohibition the wording of which was general and he may have provided a second specifying Sunna which made evidence that his order of prohibition was not intended to prohibit what he made lawful, nor that his order of permission made lawful what he had prohibited. For all the possibilities of this kind parallel examples exist in the Quran. The contradictory Sunna is due either to incomplete transmission rendering it contradictory, although what was lacking can be known from other traditions or it is the product of the transmitter's imagination. No contradictory tradition from the Prophet was known to Imam Shafi'i for which a possible explanation was lacking or the category to which it belonged was not known."

The Imam further said:

"Analogy on the basis of the Sunna falls into two categories, each sub-divided into various forms. God has imposed the obligation of obedience upon men through His book and His Prophets' tongue, in accordance with the obligation of obedience set forth in his established judgment that men shall obey his will without challenge to his command. The Holy Prophet specified the meaning of what God made obligatory or in any narrative transmitted from him so that nothing is left unexplained and the scholars are under obligation to regard this narrative as authentic as other traditions if it expresses the identical meaning. The second category of traditions consist of a general order of permission qualified by a particular order of prohibition. Men should regard all acts under the general order of permission as lawful and the specific act under the particular order of prohibition as unlawful. But in so doing they should not apply analogy to a particular order of prohibition, for the general rule is that an order of permission and analogy must be applied ordinarily on the general, not on the particular rule."

The interlocutor asked Imam Shafi'i if we find in the Quran an explicit general meaning which a certain Sunna may either make specific or to which it may give an implicit meaning that is contradictory, did he agree that the Sunna is abrogated by the Quran? The Imam replied:

"Since God has imposed on the Prophet the duty to obey his communication to him, and he testified to his right guidance and imposed on men the duty to obey him, and since the Arab tongue, as already explained, may give a variety of meanings for each word so that some of the communications of the book are general— and other particular. Sunna cannot be contradictory to the book of God, but will always follow the book of God, in conformity with his divine communication, and clarify on God's behalf the meaning intended by God. Thus Sunna always follows the book of God."

It is not possible to detail here further rules for judging the authenticity of the precepts and usages of the Holy Prophet and their interpretation, but what the great Imam has said perhaps contains the pith and substance of Ilmul-Hadith.[6]

In addition to the above, the interpreters of Quran including Islamic scholars may also apply the following rules of interpretation, expounded by modern jurists like Maxwell, to interpret this Holy scripture but they should not attempt to put their own construction in opposition to the express rulings of Muslim commentators of great antiquity and higher authority as stated above.

Literal rule of interpretation:

Interpretation is the method by which the true sense or the meaning of the word is understood. The question of interpretation can arise only if two or more possible constructions are sought to be placed on a provision-one party suggesting one construction and the other a different one. But where the parties agree on the true interpretation of a provision or do not raise any question in respect thereof, the question of further interpretation does not arise.

To find out the exact connotation of a word in a statute we must took to the context in which it is used. The context would quite often provide the key to meaning of the word and the sense it should carry. Its setting would give colour to it and provide clue to the intention of the Legislature in using it. A word, as said by Holmes, is not a crystal, transparent and unchanged; it is the skin of a living thought and may vary greatly in colour and content according to the circumstances and the time in which it is used.

The words, phrases and sentences of a statute are ordinarily to be understood in their natural, ordinary or popular and grammatical meaning unless such a construction leads to an absurdity or the context or object of the statute suggest a different meaning.

The words, phrases, and sentences of Quran are ordinarily to be understood in their natural, ordinary or popular and grammatical meaning and any subjective interpretation or any interpretation leading to absurdity must be avoided. For example, some of our Hindu brothers and sisters think that the word Kafir refers to them only and it is a word of contempt. It simply distinguishes between those who accept the faith and those who reject it. It is neither an abusive term nor an expression of condemnation.

Faith is a matter of personal conviction and as such anyone who rejects a particular religion, may be Islam, is not to be condemned, abused or persecuted for his faith or belief. Surah Al-Kafirun also gives a clear message that Kafirs (those rejecting faith) are to be treated decently and not persecuted or condemned. To quote:

1. Say: O ye
   That reject not that
2. I worship not that
   which ye worship
3. Nor will ye worship
   That which I worship.
4. And I will not worship
   That which ye have been
   Wont to worship
5. Nor will ye worship
   That which I worship.
6. To you be your Way,
   And to me mine.

Ejusdem generis. The expression means of the same kind. The phrase *ejusdem generis* is mere a rule of construction and not a rule of substantive law and is hardly applicable where the intention of the act is otherwise clear. If a general word, in other words, is added to specific words, the general word would take its colour from the specific words, and obviously when there are no specific words in the clause the rule of *ejusdem generis* will not be applicable. The essential pre-requisite of the doctrine is that there must be coupling of words together to show that they are to be understood in the same sense.

Harmonious construction. It is a cardinal rule of construction that when there are in a statute two provisions which are in conflict with each other such that both of them cannot stand, they should, if possible, be so interpreted that effect can be given to both, and that a construction which renders either of them inoperative and useless should not be adopted except in the last resort. This is what is known as the rule of harmonious construction. One application of this rule is that when there is a law generally dealing with a subject and another dealing particularly with one of the topics comprised therein, the general law is to be construed as yielding to the special in respect of the matters comprised therein. The reason of the rule requires that it should apply whenever there is overlapping of the fields occupied by two conflicting enactments, and when that is shown, it would not be logical to exclude its application on the ground that the enactments have been made with a different purpose. It is the identity of the subject-matter of the conflicting provisions, not the identity of their purpose or angle of vision that is essential for the application of the magazine.

The Muslims must also display by their conduct a correct understanding of Islamic concepts. Dr Tahir Mahmood a well-known Indian Islamic Jurist had also made a similar appeal to the Muslim Community in early eighties. To quote:

"At a seminar held on 18th October, 1980 under the auspices of the Department of Islamic and Comparative Law, Indian Institute of Islamic Studies, New Delhi, he made an appeal to the Muslim Community to display by their conduct a correct understanding of Islamic concepts on marriages and divorce."[7]

References

1. Plural of 'Hadis' which means Tradition or narration relating to or describing a saying or an action of Prophet Muhammad (BPUH).
2. Agha Mahmood Jaffer Bindanim v. Koolsoom Beebee, I.L.R. 25, Cal. 9 (P.C.).
3. Amod Giri v. Mst. Bagh, A.I.R., 1955, J & K 1.
4. Md. Ismail v. Abdul Rashid, A.I.R., 1956, All 1 (F.B.)
5. K. Veerankutty v. Pathunmakatty Umma, A.I.R., 1956, Mad 514.
6. Mst. Khurshid Jan v. Fazal Dad, 1964, PLD (W.P.) 558.
7. Islamic and Comparative Law Quarterly, April–June 1981, p.146.

6

Muslim Women's Right of Inheritance

Allah, the Exalted, stated in the Glorious Qur'an: [Allah commands you as regards to your children's (inheritance); to the male, a portion equal to that of two females.] [4:11]

Those who having misunderstood Islam feel as if Islam discriminates against women in matters of inheritance. They contend that it is unfair to grant the male a double to that of the female even though they are their own children. We find in Quran details of the shares of all the relatives in respect to their relationship to the deceased. As He the Most Wise said: (There is a share for men and a share for women from what is left by parents and those nearest related, whether the property is small or large, an obligatory share.) [4:7]

This means that the minimum of her shares is half, and considering that a female has no continual financial responsibilities as a child, sister, wife or mother, and these responsibilities are always on the men of the family. It will not be out of place to quote a famous tradition here. The companion Saad ibn Abi Waqqas was ill and requested to bequest the majority of his wealth as charity, or a half of it since he was wealthy and only had one daughter. The Prophet (Peace be upon Him) forbade him and only allowed him to give a third, and said : "A third and a third is a lot, and it is better that you leave your heirs wealthy rather than leave them needy begging from the people. You will not spend anything seeking Allah's countenance but you receive a reward for that expenditure, even the morsel of food you put into your wife's mouth." [Bukhari #2591 & Muslim #1628]

In Islam, a male is required to take care of the entire financial needs of the female dependents of the family until they are married. From the time a female marries, her financial responsibilities are her husband's obligation. After the death of the husband, the son or other male relative is obliged to care for the widow. Therefore, demanding a fair, just or equal share of inheritance for both male and female Muslims, who do not have equal financial obligations and responsibilities, is an unfair and unjust demand and the doctrine of reasonable classification may be the touchstone to test the veracity of this provision.

Gustave Le Bon, a French social psychologist, sociologist and anthropologist, says in his book on Arab Civilisation:

"The principles of inheritance which have been determined in the Qur'an have a great deal of justice and fairness. The person who reads the Qur'an can perceive these concepts of justice and fairness in terms of inheritance through the verses... I should also point out the great level of efficiency in terms of general laws and rules derived from these verses. I have compared British, French and Islamic Laws of inheritance and found that Islam grants the wives the right of inheritance, which our laws are lacking while Westerners consider them to be ill-treated by the Muslim men."

A Muslim can deal or dispose his wealth in the manner he likes but while executing a will he can give only 1/3rd of his wealth to whoever he wants but the remaining 2/3rd shall be distributed according to the Islamic law of inheritance derived from the Qur'an.

Examples showing the distribution of the estate of a deceased person (Particularly Women) professing Islam

Example 1

A man dies leaving behind two sons and two daughters and a widow.

Widow as sharer takes 1/8.

The two daughters are excluded from a share by their brothers, but come in again as residuaries in right of their brothers taking 1/2 only of what the brothers take.

Residue is 7/8.

This must be divided into six parts, two parts for each son and one part for each daughter.

Ultimate division: widow 1/8 or 6/48; each son 2/6 of 7/8 or 14/48; each daughter 1/6 of 7/8 or 7/48.

Example 2

A man dies leaving behind two widows, a mother and three sons.

The two widows take as sharers 1/8 between them.

The mother takes as sharer 1/6.

Residue is 17/24, which is divided between the three sons.

Ultimate division: each widow 9/144; mother 24/144; each son 34/144.

Example 3

A man dies leaving behind a widow, a mother, and a sister.

The widow as sharer takes 1/4 or 3/12.

The mother as sharer takes 1/3 or 4/12.

The sister as sharer takes 1/2 or 6/12.

3/12+4/12+6/12 make 13/12.

The denominator must therefore be increased to 13, that is, the property must be divided into thirteen parts instead of twelve.

Ultimate division: widow 3/13; mother 4/13; sister 6/13.

Example 4

A man dies leaving behind a widow, a father, a mother, and two daughters.

Widow as sharer takes 1/8 or 3/24.

Father as sharer takes 1/6 or 4/24.

Mother as sharer takes 1/6 or 4/24.

Two daughters as sharers take 2/3 or 16/24 between them.

3/24+4/24+4/24+16/24 make 27/24.

The denominator must therefore be increased to 27, i.e. the property must be divided into twenty-seven parts instead of twenty-four.

Ultimate division: widow 3/27; father 4/27; mother 4/27; each daughter 8/27.

Example 5

A man dies leaving behind a widow, a mother, and two sons.

The widow takes a share of 1/8.

The mother 1/6.

Residue is 17/24.

Ultimate division: widow, 6/48; mother, 8/48; each son, 17/48.

Example 6

A man dies leaving behind two daughters of a son, daughter of son's son, son of son's son's son.

Two daughters of son take as sharers 2/3.

Daughter of son's son is excluded from a sharer as 2/3 allotted to females is exhausted.

Residue is 1/3.

The residue is divided between the son of the son's son's son and the daughter of the son's son in the proportion of two to one.

Ultimate division: each daughter 1/2 of 2/3 or 6/18; son of son's son's son 2/3 of 1/3 or 4/18; daughter of son's son 1/3 of 1/3 or 2/18.

Example 7

A man dies leaving behind two daughter, a son's daughter, a son's son's daughter, and a son's son's son's son.

The two daughter take as sharers 2/3.

Residue is 2/3.

This must be divided into four parts, two for the son's son's son's son, one for the son's daughter, and one for the son's son's daughter.

Ultimate division: each daughter 4/12; son's son's son's son 2/4 of 1/3 or 2/12; son's daughter 1/4; son's son's daughter 1/4 of 1/3 or 1/12.

Example 8

A woman dies leaving behind a husband, a daughter, and a paternal uncle.

The husband as sharer takes 1/4.

The daughter as sharer takes 1/2.

Residue is 1/4 which is taken by the paternal uncle.

Ultimate division: husband 1/4; daughter 2/4; uncle 1/4.

Example 9

A woman dies leaving behind a husband, two daughter, and two sisters.

Husband takes as sharer 1/4.

Daughters take as sharers 2/3.

Residue is 1/12.

Sisters take this as residuaries with the daughters.

Ultimate division: husband 6/24; each daughter 8/24; each sister 1/2 of 1/12 or 1/24.

Example 10

A man dies leaving behind a widow, two daughters, and a paternal grandmother.

The widow takes a share of 1/8 or 3/24.

The two daughters take a share of 2/3 or 16/24 between them.

The paternal grandmother takes a share of 1/6 or 4/24.

3/24+16/24+4/24=23/24.

There is therefore a return of 1/24, which will be divided between the two daughters and the grandmother in the proportion of their shares, i.e. four to one.

Two daughter's take 4/5 of 1/24.

Grandmother takes 1/5 of 1/24.

Ultimate division: widow 1/8 or 15/120; each daughter

1/3+2/5 of 1/24 or 42/120; grandmother 21/120.

Example 11

A dies leaving behind a widow, a brother, a sister, the widow's mother, and the widow's brother. Before distribution the widow dies. On the distribution of A's property:

The widow of A gets a share of 1/4.

A's sister is excluded from a share by her brother.

The widow's mother and the widow's brother are not entitled to anything.

Residue is 3/4 which is divided between A's brother and sister in the proportion of two to one.

Ultimate division of A's property: widow of A 1/4; brother of A 2/3 of 3/4 or 2/4; sister of A 1/3 of 3/4 or 1/4.

Example 12

A dies leaving behind three sons and a daughter. Before distribution one son dies leaving a widow, two brothers, and a sister.

There are no sharers on the first distribution.

The property is divided into seven parts, of which each son takes 2/7 and the daughter 1/7.

On the second distribution the share of the deceased son, which is 2/7, is to be divided between his widow, his two brothers (sons of A) and his sister (daughter of A).

Widow of deceased son of A takes a share of 1/4 of 2/7.

Daughter of A is excluded by her brothers (sons of A).

The residue, which is 3/4 of 2/7, is divided between the sons of A and the daughter of A.

Sons of A take 4/5 of 3/4 of 2/7 or 24/120.

Daughter of A takes 1/5 of 3/4 of 2/7 or 6/120.

Ultimate division: widow of deceased son of A 10/120; each surviving son of A 2/7+12/140 or 52/140; daughter of A 1/7+6/140 or 26/140.

Example 13

A woman dies leaving behind a sister, her father's mother, her mother's mother, and her husband.

The husband takes a share of 1/4.

The father's mother and mother's mother (both true grandmothers) take a share of 1/6 between them.

The sister takes a share of 1/2.

Residue is 1/12, and as there are no residuaries this is divided between the grandmothers and the sister in proportion to their shares.

Sister by the return takes 2/3 of 1/12.

Grandmothers by the return take 1/3 of 1/12 between them.

Ultimate division: husband 18/72; sister 1/2+2/3 of 1/12 or 40/72; each grandmother 7/72.

Comparison between Sunni and Shia Laws of Inheritance:

Sunni and Shia laws of inheritance are different though both the laws are based on Quranic injunctions. In India Sunnis are in majority and that is the reason our legal literature generally covers Sunni law of inheritance.

Classes of Legal Heirs:

Shia law divides legal heirs into three basic classes. These classes are categorised as under:

Class 1:

(i) Parents, and
(ii) Children (male and female). The children also include their descendant show low so ever irrespective of the fact whether they are descendants of male or female children.

Class 2:

(i) Grandparents (true or false) how high soever, and

(ii) Brothers and sisters (full, consanguine, and uterine) and their descendant show low soever irrespective of their gender.

Class 3:

(i) Paternal uncles and aunts,

(ii) Maternal uncles and aunts, and

(iii) Their children how low soever irrespective of their gender. Once the heirs are divided into the above classes, there are two basic rules which need to be understood.

Firstly, as long as an heir (or more than one) is present from the class 1, no one will be entitled to inheritance from the class 2: similarly, if there is an heir (or more than one) from the class 2, no will have anything from the class 3. These classes lay down a basic framework in which an estate of a Shia deceased is distributed except that deceased's spouse is dealt with differently.

Secondly, within the same class there is no difference between male and female heirs except to the extent that a male heir will have double share than that of a female heir. For instance, descendants of a Sunni deceased's daughter are excluded from inheritance as per Sunni law as they are regarded as distant kindred whose right to inheritance will only be entertained in absence of the sharers and the residuaries, while his son's descendants will be entitled to his estate as they are regarded as the sharer or the residuary. Shia law does not differentiate between descendants of son and daughter and they are placed in the same class.

According to Sunni law, legal heirs are divided into three classes, i.e. the sharers, the residuaries and the distant kindred; while Shia law recognises only two classes, i.e. the sharers and the residuaries. There is no concept of distant kindred in Shia law. Most of those who are regarded as distant kindred in Sunni law relate to a deceased from his female descendants (e.g. daughter's children, son's daughter's children) or other female relatives (e.g. mother's father, mother's brother and sister, sister's children etc.).

As is apparent from the above classification, there is no such distinction in Shia law. Both paternal and maternal grandfathers are placed in the same class. If a deceased leaves behind a daughter and a grandson, in Sunni law, the daughter will have half of the estate while the rest will be inherited by the grandson as a residuary. The situation will be different in Shia law because of variant application of the rule the nearer in degree will exclude the remoter in degree. Shia law is similar with Sunni law to some extent and dissimilar to another extent with respect to distribution of an estate among brothers of different kinds, i.e. full, consanguine and uterine. Full brother excludes consanguine brother, but neither full nor consanguine brother exclude uterine brother. In Sunni law, full sister does not exclude consanguine brother.

As far as the class 3 of legal heirs in Shia law is concerned which includes paternal and maternal uncles and aunts and their descendants, there is no preference on the basis that someone is linked to a deceased from paternal or maternal side.

Inheritance of Spouses:

As is apparent from the above three-fold classification of heirs in Shia law, spouses are not placed in anyone of them. The above referred classes are jointly known as heirs by consanguinity in Shia law, while spouses are termed as heirs by affinity. The heirs by consanguinity are also termed as heirs by *Nasab*, while the heirs by affinity are heirs by *Sabab*. Thus, husband and wife form an independent category similar to Sunni law which is only affected by presence or absence of deceased's children. If there are children of a deceased, husband or wife will inherit 1/4 or 1/8 respectively. But if a deceased dies issueless, husband or wife will have 1/2 or 1/4 respectively. If a deceased husband leaves behind more than one wife as legal heirs, they will share jointly in their prescribed share, i.e. 1/4 or 1/8.

There is one important distinction between Shia and Sunni laws regarding the inheritance of childless widow. In the former law, she is not entitled to land or immovable property though she has a right to her prescribed share from her deceased husband's movable assets.

Principle of Representation:

Both the schools agree that heirs of a predeceased heir will not inherit anything if other heirs of the deceased are alive.

Rule of Radd/Return:

When an entire estate of a Shia Muslim is not consumed by his/her heirs and something is left out of it, the rule of Radd/return is applied as is done in Sunni law. The application of Radd is more frequent in Shia law because it accords less significance to Ausbaat/residuaries as compared to Sunni law. In Sunni law an exhaustive list of the residuaries reduces the occurrences of application of Radd. Whenever there is residue of an estate of a deceased Sunni Muslim that will be given to any eligible residuary irrespective of the fact how remotely he is related to the deceased. While such an exhaustive list is not available in Shia law and even those who are regarded as the residuaries they cannot operate beyond the sphere of their own basic class.

Principle of Aul/Increase:

The principle of Aul is not recognised in Shia law of inheritance and Shia scholars have expounded rules to avoid its application. In Sunni law, whenever the calculated shares of heirs of a deceased are increased from the supposed shares of that estate, the supposed shares are increased to match the number of the calculated shares.

(Above details have been derived from authentic sources, a few mentioned here, after consulting relevant material on the subject and reproduced, in an abbreviated form. However, persons belonging to some other schools of thought, not so common in India, may not agree with some of the observations as they have their own convictions which they are at liberty to have and follow. Our purpose is neither to support nor condemn any school of thought. Our only purpose is to narrate what is handy and by and large applicable in this part of the sub-continent. Those interested in further details may refer to the books mentioned below:—

1. Sir William Markby, a Former Judge of Calcutta High Court in pre-partition India "HINDU AND MAHOMMEDAN LAW."

2. Sir R.K.Wilson's *Digest of Anglo- Muhammedan Law*, Sec. 227.
3. Coulson, N.J. *Succession in the Muslim Family* (Cambridge University Press, London 1971).
4. Verma, B. R. Mohammadan *Law in India and Pakistan* (Law Publishers, Allahabad 1962).
5. Purohit, N. *The Principles of Mohammedan Law* (2nd Edition) (Orient Publishing Company, New Delhi 1998).
6. Ameer Ali *Commentaries on Mahommedan Law*.
7. Fyzee, A. A. A. *Outlines of Muhammadan Law* (Edited by Tahir Mahmood).

   (Oxford University Press, New Delhi 2009).
8. Mulla, D. F. Principles of Mahommedan Law.
9. Al-Sabooni, M. A. Al-Muwarith fi al-Shariah al-Islamia fi Zuo al-Kitab ws Sunnah (Inheritance in Islamic Shariah in light of the Quran and Sunnah) (Dar-ul-Qalam, Damascus).
10. Khan, H. *The Islamic Law of Inheritance*: A Comparative Study of Recent Reforms in Muslim Countries (Oxford University Press, Karachi 2007).
11. Al Sirajiyyah or *The Mahommedan Law of Inheritance* as Translated by William Jones (Edited by Almaric Rumsey)
12. Saksana, K. P. Muslim Law As *Administered in India and Pakistan* (Eastern Book Company, Lucknow 1963).

7

Adoption of Male/Female Child

Islam does not recognise the institution of adoption. Marriage of the Prophet Mohammad was solemnised with Zainab after being divorced by Zaid. Zaid belonged to the tribe of Kalb, and was a slave of the lady Khadija, the Prophet's first wife. The Holy Prophet liberated Zaid, and got him married to his cousin Zainab. The marriage failed and so the Prophet's efforts for a reconciliation. Zaid on account of his great attachment to the Prophet was called a "Son of Mohammad." The Holy Quran refers to this incident.

"And when you said to him (Zaid) whom Allah had shown favour and you have favoured "keep your wife to yourself and fear Allah," but you concealed in your heart what Allah would disclose, and you feared men while Allah was worthier to be feared therefore, when Zaid had accomplished his want of her. We gave her to you, as a wife so that there should be no difficulty for the believers to marry the wives of their adopted sons when they have divorced them, and Allah's command shall be performed." Part. XXXVII. Ch., XXXIII.

In Quran (XXXIII:4), that 'God has not made your adopted sons your natural sons'. It is what you say Allah conveys truth only and it is the proper track to move on.

The courts in India have also taken the same view. Cases, cited below, bear testimony thereto:

The custom of adoption: The custom of adoption was prevalent in pre-Islamic Arabia. A son was adopted by contract with the parents.

The system seems to have received some recognition by the adoption of Zaid. It was, however, abrogated by a verse of the Quran[1] and the bar to the marriage of the Prophet with the divorced of Zaid was removed. Adoption, such as, is known to Hindu Law, creating a relationship of parentage, is unknown to Mohammedan Law. It does not recoginse this mode of affiliation[2] as it was positively forbidden by the Quran. The whole Muslim jurisprudence being based on different conception of legitimacy, adoption must be out of place in it.[3] Adoption does not confer any rights of inheritance or other rights on the adopted son.[4]

The custom of adoption prevails among many clases of Mohammedans in India and in some cases converts from Hinduism have retained the custom of adoption. But there is no presumption that a Hindu convert to Islam has retained such custom. The burden of proving that such custom has been retained lies on those who assert it.[5] Such customs are prevailing in the Punjab,[6] Sindh[7] and Ajmer High Courts.[8] Customs on the subject will prevail over Mohammedan Law except to the extent to which they have been abrogated by Sec. 3 (1) of the Shariat Act (See Sec. 2, N. 13). If a declaration is made as required by the section, the custom of adoption shall become ineffective.[9]

Adoption and doctrine of acknowledgement: In the Full Bench decision of Allahabad High Court rendered by Justice Mahmood in Muhammad Allahadad Khan v. Muhammad Ismail Khan[10], it was pointed out that while among the Muslims there is doctrine of acknowledgement of paternity there is no question of adoption in Muslim Law. This is also the view expressed in Mulla's Muslim Law, vide Chapter XVII and in the Principles of Mohammedan Law by Amir Ali, vide Part II, Chapter.[11] Tahir Mahmood is also of the view that in Muslim Law the term 'Walad' (child) means only a child by birth no other form of 'fronship' is recognised by Muslim Law.[12]

Shariyat and religious text on adoption: Muslim Law in its pure form governed by Shariyat or Hidaya does not recognise the principle of adoption,—There is no controversy between the parties that adoption in not an absolute anthema to the Muslim community in

Rajasthan. Undoubtedly, the Muslim Law in its pure form governed by Shariyat or Hidaya does not recognise the principle of adoption. However, wherever there exists a custom amongst the Muslim community whether by way of a family custom or by way of community custom or by way of regional custom permitting adoption amongst Muslim, such adoption has been recognised by the courts in India.[13]

Adoption and sanction of law: In certain cases the right of adoption is allowed by law. Thus a taluqdar in Oudh is permitted by Section 29 of the Oudh Estates Act, to adopt a son.[14] These laws have not been superseded by Shariat Act.

Under the juvenile justice law in India Muslims, too, can adopt a child but the doctrine of acknowledgement of paternity shall continue to apply. However, as stated above, wherever there exists a custom amongst the Muslim community whether by way of a family custom or by way of community custom or by way of regional custom permitting adoption amongst Muslim, such adoption has been recognised by the courts in India.

References

1. Quran, 33, 39.
2. Mohd. Umar v Mohd. Niazuddin, I.L.R. 39 Cal. 418:13 I.C. 344:39 I.A. 19; Mir Zaman v Nur Alam, A.I.R. 1936 Pesh. 108 at p. 108: 162 I.C. 314; Nazir Khan v Ganesh. A.I.R. 1926 All. 687: 96 I.C. 617; Mohd. Allahadad v Mohd. Islam, I.L.R. 10 All. 289.
3. Habibur Rahman v Altaf Ali, A.I.R. 1922 P.C. 159 at p. 161.
4. Mohd. Allahadad v Mohd. Islam, I.L.R. 10 All. 289 at p. 340.
5. Bai Machhbai v Bai Hirbai, I.L.R. 36 Bom. 264: 10 I.C. 816 (Girasis of Bombay).
6. Khair Ali Shah v Imam Shah, A.I.R. 1936 Lah. 80 at p. 81.
7. Usman v Asat, A.I.R. 1925 Sind. 207.
8. Abdullah Khan v Sunda, 11 I.C. 670.
9. Ayubsha v Babalal, A.I.R. 1938 Bom. 111 at p. 113: I.L.R. (1938) Bom. 150.
10. (1888) I.L.R. 10 All. 290.
11. Mohd. Aliqu Khan v Union of India, 2003 All. L.J. 2268 at p. 2269.

12. Tohir Mahmood and saif Mahmood Muslim Law in India and abroad p. 197.
13. 1. L. Rs. of Allahdeen v Board of Revenue, 2007 (1) R.L.R. 582 at p. 587 (Raj.)
14. Abdul Halim v Saadat Ali Khan, A.I.R. 1932 P.C. 137 at p. 138: I.L.R. 7 Luck. 194; on appeal from A.I.R. 1929 Oudh 126; Mohd. Azim Khan v Raja Saadat Ali Khan, A.I.R. 1931 Oudh 177: 136 I.C. 642: 8 C.W.N. 349.

8

Islam Discourages Polygamy and Divorce

It looks yellow to the jaundiced eye and as such those with a bias feel and propagate that Muslims are a Polygamous community though ground situation has a different story to tell and the religious scriptures also contain provisions just contrary to it. Muslims are not a polygamous sect.

The development of the institution of marriage is a matter of historical interest. It originated in the form of irregular unions and marital unions.[1]

Polyandry, polygamy and even monogamy were enjoined by immemorial customs and practised in different parts of the world. Polygamy and plurality of wives is permissible in Islam but it prefers monogamy. Those who feel that polygamy is an Islamic concept are ill-informed. The fact is that Islam inherited the doctrine of plurality of wives from time immemorial. Many a Prophet had married a number of wives. Jacob had Joseph and his brothers born of different wives, the Prophet Solomon had contracted numerous marriages. Abraham, the traditional founder of the Quresh Arabs, had at least two wives. Even prior to Islam, Polygamy was customary among ancient Arabs and they could have as many wives as they liked. It was practised by the Jews and the 'ancient' Christian Church did not forbid it. However, the Romans later on preferred monogamy, and it was a fundamental rule of Roman law that a man could not have two wives at the same time "*duos uxores eoden tempore habere non licet.*" The Hindu Law did not restrict the number of wives till the Hindu

Marriage Act, 1955 was enacted. The only verse of Quran that deals with plurality of wives is Surah 4:3.

To quote:

"Marry such women as seem good
to you, two, three or four; but if you
fear that you cannot do justice (between
them) then marry only one."

"And it is not in your power to do
justice between wives, even though you
may covet it; but keep yourself not
aloof from one with total aversion, nor
leave her like one in suspense, and if
you make reconciliation, and guard
yourself, then surely Allah is Forgiving,
Merciful."

The view that Islam allows four wives at a time for sheer sensual pleasure is just contrary to what is ordained in Quran.

"Even during the last century the great jurist Ameer Ali had said:

'The conviction is gradually forcing itself on all sides, in all Moslem communities, that polygamy is much opposed to Islamic laws as it is to the general progress of civilised society and true culture. In consequence of this conviction a large and growing section of Islamists regards the practice of polygamy as positively unlawful.'"

As interpreted by courts and Muslim jurists the purport of the said verse can be understood and appreciated in the context of the ill-treatment meted out to the orphans by the Arabs. After the death of the father his brothers or uncles and other near relatives, used to take into possession the property of the children of the deceased, and did not return it to them even after they attained majority. They used to misappropriate their good cattle and give in exchange lean and emaciated cattle from their own herd. Sometimes, they would mix the property of the orphans with their own properties and misappropriate the same. They would marry the female orphans without payment of dower according to their status and were not particular about discharging their liabilities towards them since they were friendless.

As mentioned in chapter 1, Muslim Law permits polygamy but has never encouraged it. The sanction for polygamy among Muslim is traced to the Quran IV. 3—

"If ye fear that ye cannot do justice between orphans. Then marry what seems good to you of women, by twos, threes or fours or if ye fear that ye cannot be equitable, then only one, or what your right hand possesses. This is more proper that you may do justice."

"It is admitted on all hands that this chapter was revealed to guide the Muslims under the conditions which followed the battle of Uhud......"

(The Holy Quran by Maulana Muhammad Ali). In another passage the Quran says:

"Ye are never able
To be fair and just
As between women,
Even if it is
Your ardent desire:
............................" (Chapter IV., Verse 129.)

V. R. Krishna Iyer, a former Judge of the Supreme Court of India, has, in his book titled "The Dialectics & Dynamics of Human Rights in India (Yesterday, Today and Tomorrow– p. 129) has rightly said that Quranic injunction has to be understood in the perspective of prevalent unrestricted polygamy and in the context of the battle in which most males perished, leaving many females or orphans and that the Holy Prophet himself recognised the difficulty of treating two or more wives with equal justice and, in such a situation, directed that an individual should have only one wife. In short, the Quran enjoined monogamy upon Muslims and departure therefrom as an exception. That is why, in the true spirit of the Quran, a number of

Muslim countries have codified the personal law wherein the practice of polygamy has been either totally prohibited or severely restricted."[2]

World historians have apprised the whole world that in Arabia the process of the subjection of the women and children was totally complete before the dawn of Islam, and the endeavours of the Prophet of God were to emancipate the woman from hereditary bondage, restore her position, and grant her a legal status.

The Fatawa-i-Alamgiri and The Siraj-ul-wahaj sum up thus:

'Marriage legalises the mutual enjoyment of the parties in a manner permitted by law, thus says the Fath-el-kadir. It imposes on the husband the obligation of dower, of maintaining and clothing her. It establishes on both sides the prohibition of affinity and the right of inheritance. It obliges the husband to be just between his wives, and to have due regard to their respective rights. It imposes on the wives the duty of obedience, and the husband is enjoined to treat them with courtesy and kindness.'

It will not be out of place to mention here that during aiyam-i-jahiliyat, that is, the times or days of ignorance or paganism (the times previous to the manifestation of Islam), one could have as many wives as he liked. As a matter of fact Islamic injunction was really a restrictive measure and reduced the number of wives to four at a time: it imposed a ceiling on conjugal greed which prevailed among males on an extensive scale. The right to four wives appears to have been qualified by "better not" advice, and husbands were enjoined to restrict themselves to one wife if they could not be impartial between several wives–an impossible condition according to several Muslim jurists, who rely on it for their argument that Muslim law in practice discourages polygamy.

A Muslim has the undisputed legal right to take as many as four wives at a time. But it does not follow that Muslim law in India gives no right to the first wife against a husband who takes a second wife, or that this law renders her helpless when faced with the prospect of sharing her husband's consortium with another woman. In India, a Muslim wife can divorce her husband, under his delegated power in the event of his taking a second wife.[3]

In John Jiban Chandra v. Abinash Chandra Sen (A.I.R. 1939, Cal. 417) it was held that the second marriage is a valid marriage where it was performed after conversion to Mohammadanism of an Indian Christian domiciled in India even though his first wife an Indian Christian domiciled in India was living as wife at the time of second marriage.

Again a Muslim wife can stipulate for the power to divorce herself in case of the husband availing of his legal right to take another wife.[4] In Ayatunnessa Beebee v. Karam Ali (I. L. R. 36, Cal. 23) it was held that a Muslim wife, who has the power given to her by the marriage contract to divorce herself in the event of the husband taking a second wife does not lose her option by failing to exercise it the very moment she knows that he has done so, for "a second marriage is not a single but a continuing wrong to the first wife."

The court significantly described a second marriage as a "continuing wrong" to the first wife. The implications of these rights of the first wife are unmistakable. To say the least, a law cannot regard the husband's right to compel all his wives to submit to his consortium as fundamental and inviolate if it permits a wife to make a stipulation that she will break up her marriage on his taking a second wife. Further, the moral foundation of this right is considerably weakened if the law, while tolerating it, calls "continuing wrong" to the first wife and permits her to stipulate that she will repudiate her marriage vows on the coming of a second wife.

If Muslim law had regarded a polygamous husband's right to consortium with the first wife as fundamental and inviolate, it would have banned such stipulations by the wife as against Muslim public policy. But it has done no such thing. On the contrary Muslim law has conferred upon the wife's stipulated right to dissolve her marriage on her husband taking a second wife a force overriding the sanctity of the first marriage itself.

If Mohammedan Law permits and enforces such agreements it follows that it prefers the breaking up of the first marriage to compel the first wife to share her husband with the second. The general law, too, recognises the sanctity of such agreements, and it has been held that a contract restraining a Muslim husband from entering into a second marriage during the lifetime of the first is not void under Section 23 of the Contract Act which bans agreements in restraint of marriage.

Muslim law as enforced in India has considered polygamy as an institution to be tolerated but not encouraged, and has not conferred upon the husband any fundamental right to compel the first wife to share his consortium with another woman in all circumstances. A Muslim husband has the legal right to take a second wife even while the first marriage subsists, but if he does so, and then seeks the assistance of the Civil Court to compel the first wife to live with him against her wishes on pain of severe penalties including attachment of property, she is entitled to raise the question whether the Court, as a Court of equity, ought to compel her to submit to co-habitation with such a husband. In that case the circumstances in which his second marriage took place are relevant and material in deciding whether his conduct in taking a second wife was in itself an act of cruelty to the first.

It is not correct to say that the first wife is in no case entitled to consider the second marriage as an act of cruelty to her. Shamsunnissa Begum's case (11 M.I.A. 551) the Privy Council observed that "the Mohammedan Law, on a question of what is legal cruelty between man and wife, would probably not differ materially from the English law." It follows that Indian law does not recognise various types of cruelty such as "Muslim" cruelty, "Christian" cruelty, "Hindu" cruelty and so on, and that the test of cruelty is based on universal and humanitarian standards that is to say conduct of the husband which would cause such bodily or mental pain as to endanger the wife's safety or health.

What the Court will regard as cruel conduct depends upon the prevailing social conditions.

Equality among Wives

It is quite evident from the quotations from Quran and the case law that polygamy is not permitted in all circumstances. It is an exception; not a rule. It was permitted only to safeguard the rights of orphans. Moreover, in case of more than one marriage there should be complete equality between the wives. An absolute justice in the matter of feelings of love, emotions and affection is clearly impossible and it is, undoubtedly, an impracticable proposition. It acts as a rider and in the legal terminology, it may be termed as a proviso converting the permission into prohibition. Thus, Islam does not grant unfettered liberty for practising polygamy. Just see how difficult it is to meet the following conditions as per Deobandi School of thought:

1. If a person has more than one wife it is wajib (obligatory) upon him to treat each one equally. Whatever he gives to one wife, the other wife also has the right to claim something equal to that in value. This rule of equality applies to all types of wives, i.e. whether both were virgins at the time of marriage, both were previously married or one was a virgin at the time of marriage while the other had been previously married. If he spends one night with one wife, he will have to spend one night with the other wife as well. If he spends two or three nights with one wife, he will have to do the same with the other wife as well. Whatever wealth, jewellery, clothes, etc. he gives to one wife, the other wife also has the right to claim something equal to that in value.

2. If a person marries a second woman, the rights of this new wife and the rights of the old wife are the same. There is no difference in rights between the two.

3. Equality is based on spending the night and it is not necessary to spend an equal time with them during the day. If a person spends more time with one wife during the day and less time with the other, there is no harm in this. However, it is wajib to spend an equal time with them at night. If a person goes to one wife immediately after maghrib, and the following day he goes to the other wife after isha, he will be sinning. However, if a person's occupation is such that he works at night and remains at home during the day; for him, the basis of equality will be the day. For example, a night watchman or guard will have to base his equality with his wives according to the day and not the night.

4. There is no equality in engaging in sexual intercourse in the sense that if a person engages in sexual intercourse with one wife, it is not necessary for him to engage in sexual intercourse with the other wife as well.

5. The man has to maintain equality in allocating nights to his wives irrespective of whether he is ill or not.

6. There is no sin in loving one wife more than the other because these matters are connected to the heart and one does not have any control over one's heart.

7. Equality is not wajib when embarking on a journey. The husband can take whichever wife he wishes. However, it is preferable to cast a lot and to take the wife in whose favour the lot was drawn. In this way there will be no unhappiness or disgruntlement.

Many Muslim countries as also some Non-Muslim countries have framed various laws with regard to Bigamy/Polygamy, a few mentioned below:

Pakistan & Bangladesh

Pakistan Government had also brought legislation in the form of 'The Muslim Family Laws Ordinance, 1961, and incorporated a provision prohibiting polygamy except with the permission of Arbitration Council. To quote:

"6. Polygamy: (i) No man, during the subsistence of an existing marriage shall, except with the previous permission in writing of the Arbitration council, contract another marriage, nor shall any such marriage contracted without such permission be registered under the Muslim Marriages and Divorces (Registration) Act, 1974.

(ii) An application for permission under sub-section (1) shall be submitted to the Chairman in the prescribed manner, together with the prescribed fee, and shall state the reasons for the proposed marriage, and whether the consent of the existing wife or wives has been obtained thereto.

(iii) On receipt of the application under sub-section (2), the Chairman shall ask the applicant and his existing wife or wives each to nominate a representative, and the Arbitration Council so constituted may, if satisfied that the proposed marriage is necessary and just, grant, subject to such conditions, if any, as may be deemed fit, the permission applied for.

(iv) In deciding the application the Arbitration Council shall record its reasons for the decision, and any party may, in the prescribed manner, within the prescribed period and on payment of the prescribed fee, prefer an application for revision, (to the Collector) concerned and his decision shall be final and shall not be called in question in any Court.

(v) Any man who contracts another marriage without the permission of the Arbitration Council shall—

(a) pay immediately the entire amount of the dower, whether prompt or deferred, due to the existing wife or wives, which amount if not so paid, shall be recoverable as arrears of land revenue; and

(b) on conviction upon complaint be punishable with simple imprisonment which may extend to one year, or with fine which may extend to five thousand rupees, or with both."

Brief history of this ordinance also deserves appreciation.

Brief History

By virtue of the Ordinance making Power Field Marshal Muhammad Ayub Khan on 2nd March, 1961 promulgated this Ordinance to implement the recommendations of the Commission on family Laws. The Commission headed by Dr Khalifa Shujauddin was formed on 4th August, 1954 to report on Marriage and Family laws of Muslims and to examine whether the existing laws governing the marriage, divorce, maintenance and ancillary matters among Muslims require any modification in order to give women their proper place in society according to fundamentals of Islam. But the President of the Commission had died before the conclusion of the deliberations and Mian Sir Abdur Rashid, Retired Chief Justice of Pakistan Federal court was appointed in his place who submitted the report on 1st June, 1956.

The Commission was composed of three men, three women and one religious scholar (to represent Ulema). The report represented by the recommendations of six lay-men majority. However, shortly thereafter in August, 1956 Moulana Ihtishamul Huq (Thanvi), a religious Scholar and a traditionalist published a vigorous dissenting report taking issue with virtually every major recommendation of his colleagues of the Commission. There then ensued an extended debate between the modernists and traditionalists.

It appears that as a result of countrywide protest of the Ulema the said report remained lying dormant with government for several years. It, however, received an impetus during the military rule of Field Marshal Muhammad Ayub Khan who could impose it on the Muslims of Pakistan under the cover of Martial Law. Regarding the enforcement of the recommendations of the Commission President Muhammad Ayub Khan in "Friends Not Masters", a book of his political auto-biography commented that "...The previous government avoided the responsibility of implementing the report through their fear of the Ulema. I had the report examined by distinguished jurists including Justice Muhammad Ibrahim of East Pakistan and Manzur Quadir, ex-Chief Justice of the High Court of West Pakistan. The recommendations of the commission did not interfere in any way with any Islamic injunction on the subject, they only provided a procedure for the proper and judicious implementation of Islamic Principles relating to marriage. I decided to implement the procedure recommended by the Commission, because, I considered it my duty as Muslim and as a Head of the State to do what was necessary to eliminate a grave social malpractice which was affecting the lives of the people.

Whether the Ordinance is opposed to the Holy Quran and Sunnah is yet to be decided by the courts of law. Dr Tanzil-ur-Rahman, Justice of Karachi High Court while delivering judgment in the case of Shawkat Hussain V. Mst. Rubina and others, held that no one can claim that Muslim Family Laws Ordinance was ever placed or discussed before National Assembly or by any Parliament under the constitution of 1962, 1972 or 1973 of or after its revival under the Presidential Order 14 of 1985. So the basis and fundamental process of legislation in democracy was always denied to this Ordinance". In Pakistan, the Ordinance was made a protected piece of legislation by including it in the first schedule of the constitution so as to save it from being challenged in a court of law on the ground that it infringed fundamental rights of the Muslims to profess and practice their religion. But after the insertion of 2-A, The Objectives Resolution to form part of substantial provision by the Presidential Order No. 4 on 2nd March, 1985 to the constitution it would not perhaps be possible to extend recognition to the said protection in so far it derogates or comes into conflict with the principles and provisions underlying the Objectives Resolutions which would ultimately affect religio-socio guarantee given to the people of Pakistan which the constitution so solemnly proclaims, envisages and secures.

Bangladesh Government had also brought similar legislation to put restrictions on POLYGAMY. Rule 14 of Muslim Family laws Rules (Bangladesh) bears testimony to it. To quote.

"14 In considering whether another proposed marriage is just and necessary during the continuance of an existing marriage, the Arbitration Council may, without prejudice to its general powers to consider what is just and necessary, have regard to such circumstances, as the following amongst others:

Sterility, physical infirmity, physical unfitness for the conjugal relation, willful avoidance of a decree for restitution of conjugal rights, or insanity on the part of an existing wife."

Other Muslim countries have also followed suit. In India, polygamy is permissible under the present laws but Indian Muslims, too, prefer monogamy and practice it exceptionally rather rarely. Now polygamy amongst Muslims is neither a practice nor a rule; it is an exception and those who deny it, deny the real ground situation and are in an illusory world. But at the same time it can not be denied that the concept of marriage, as "the voluntary union for life of one man and one woman to the exclusion of all others" is not applicable in Islam and the Muslim law considers polygamy as lawful. Thus, the Muslim ideas of matrimony are not in harmony with the Roman, Christian, or the present day Hindu concept of marriage but the view that Islam allows four wives at a time for sheer sensual pleasure is just contrary to what is ordained in Quran.

"Even during the last century the great jurist Ameer Ali had said":

"The conviction is gradually forcing itself on all sides, in all Moslem communities, that polygamy is much opposed to Islamic laws as it is to the general progress of civilised society and true culture. In consequence of this conviction a large and growing section of Islamists regards the practice of polygamy as positively unlawful."

Algeria

According to Article 8 of the Code of Family Law 1984, it is permitted to contract marriage with more than one wife within the limits of the Shariat if: (a) there is a just ground for it, (b) the legal condition of equal justice can be fulfilled, and (c) the previous and future wives are duly informed of and agree to it. The first wife can bring legal action against the husband for divorce if the second was kept in the dark about the first marriage.

Iraq

According to Article 3 of the Code of Personal Status 1959, marriage with more than one wife is not permissible except with the permission of the court and the grant of such permission shall depend on whether the husband's financial position is sound enough to support the family of more than one wife; and whether any lawful purpose would be served by such an action.

Where injustice between the wives is feared, plurality of wives will not be permissible; and determination of this fact lies with the court.

All those who procure a second marriage in contravention of these provisions shall be liable to imprisonment for a period not exceeding one year, or to fine not exceeding one hundred Dinars, or to both.

These provisions shall not apply to marriage with a widow.

Jordan

According to Article 19 of the Code of Personal Status 1976, where the wife has stipulated for something that gives her a right that the husband shall not marry another woman the conditions shall be valid and obligatory and if the husband does not fulfill them the wife can apply for a divorce.

Libya

According to Article 13 of the Family Law 1984, a married man who wants to marry again must obtain prior consent of the court. The court can give consent after examining the relevant social, financial and health factors.

Morocco

According to Article 42 of the Code of Personal Status 2004, a stipulation in the marriage contract against bigamy by the husband will be binding on him. In the absence of such a stipulation, if he wants to re-marry he must apply to the court for permission giving his reasons for it and a statement of his financial capacity.

According to Article 46, if permission for second marriage is granted, the court shall inform the woman with whom the second marriage is to be contracted that the husband is already married and has accepted all the directions given by the court under Articles 44 and 45.

Singapore

In Singapore, a married Muslim man wanting to marry again must obtain prior permission of the court which can be given on certain grounds and subject to specified conditions.

Somalia

In Somalia, a married man wanting to marry again must obtain prior permission of the court which can be given on certain grounds and subject to specified conditions.

Syria

According to Article 17 of the Code of Personal Status 1953, the court shall not permit a married man to marry again unless there is some legal justification for it and he is capable of maintaining two wives.

Tunisia

According to Article 18 of the Code of Personal Status 1956, plurality of wives is prohibited. Any person who, being already married and before the marriage is lawfully dissolved, marries again shall be liable to imprisonment for one year or for a fine of 2,40,000 Malims [Francs], or to both, even if the second marriage is in violation of any requirement of this Code.

Any person who has married in violation of the provisions laid down in Law No. 3 of 1957 relating to Organisation of Civil Status and contracts a second marriage while living in matrimony with the first wife shall be liable to the same punishment.

A person who knowingly marries someone liable to punishment under the forgoing clauses shall also be liable to the same punishment.

Turkey

In Turkey, under the Civil Code of 1926, bigamy is altogether prohibited and punishable in law.

Indonesia

According to Article 3 of the Law of Marriage 1974, in principle a man shall be allowed to have only one wife and a woman only one husband. The court may, however, grant permission to a man to have more than one wife if his first wife: (i) is unable to perform her duties as wife, or (ii) is suffering from a physical defect or incurable disease, or (iii) is incapable of having children.

Malaysia

According to Article 23 of the Islamic Family Law Act, 1984, no man, during the subsistence of a marriage, shall except with the prior permission in writing of the Shariah Judge, contract another marriage, nor shall another marriage contracted without such permission be registered under this Act.

Philippines

According to Article 162 of the Code of Muslim Personal Law 1977, any Muslim husband desiring to contract a subsequent marriage shall, before doing so, file a written notice thereof with the Clerk of the Shariah Circuit Court of the place where the family resides. Upon receipt of said notice the Clerk shall serve a copy thereof to the wife or wives. Should any of them object, an Agama [religious scholars] Arbitration Council shall be constituted in accordance with Article 161(2) above. If the Agama Arbitration Council does not get wife's consent to the proposed marriage the court shall decide whether or not to sustain her objection.

According to Article 183, a person who fails to comply with the requirements of Articles 85, 161 and 162 of this Code shall be penalised by imprisonment or a fine of two hundred to two thousand pesos, or both.

References

1. "Marital unions are the outcome of sexual selection and restrictives" *Vinogradoff Historical Jurisprudence* Vol. I., p. 167.
2. 1970 Ker. LT 4 at page 10 per Krishna Iyer, J.
3. Badu Mia v. *Badrunnessa*, I.L.R. 1919, Cal. 511 (2) at p. 518: 40 I.C. 803.
4. Sheikh Mohd v. Badrunnissa Bibee, 7 Beng. L.R. App 5 (sic); Badrunnissa Bibi v. Mafiattalla, 7 Beng, LR. 442.

9

Attributes of an ideal husband as per religious, secular and ethical parameters

While pondering over the issue as to what qualities an ideal Muslim husband must possess I could gather only the information reproduced or mentioned below, from different religious, theological, secular and ethical digital and non-digital sources. The following information which (of course not all attributes) may be quite relevant for all husbands irrespective of the religion they profess and/or even for those who have no interest in religious dictates and simply believe in ethical and moral values for being practiced in all walks of life. As regards a Muslim husband, he must possess the following qualities, which may be described as qualities of head and heart, for being a responsible and dutiful husband so that he may not take undue advantage of the liberal provisions in Muslim law, particularly in matters of marriage and divorce:

(a) The husband should be generous and affectionate with his wife. Every human being is love hungry. Love begets love. It is the key to harmonious matrimonial relationship. Warmth of the husband leads to reciprocal response from the other side.

(b) It is the duty of a Muslim husband that he should make his wife feel secure, happy and satisfied. She should not be threatened with warnings of divorce on one pretext or the other and that, too, without any cogent reason or reasons. Such statements are addressed to good people. Quran also says so:

"Good statements are for good people (or good women for good men) and good people for good statements (or good men for good women)" [Surah al-Noor 24:26].

(c) She should be treated properly. She should not be subject to cruel treatment and domestic violence. The following real story throws light on the subject:

"If two men come to propose marriage to one woman, and they are equal in terms of religious commitment, then preference should be given to the one who comes from a good family. Good family is one that adheres to moral standards and behaves properly. It may not necessarily be a rich family because the righteousness of the husband's close relatives and the family values pass on to their children and they do not resort to improper treatment even in abnormal and compelling situations. It is good if he has sufficient wealth to maintain his family because the Prophet (peace be upon him) said to Faatimah bint Qays (may Allah be pleased with her), when she came to consult him about three men who had proposed marriage to her, "As for Mu'aawiyah, he is a poor man who has no wealth..." (Narrated by Muslim, 1480). It is not essential that he should be a businessman or rich, it is sufficient for him to have an income that will keep him and his family from having to ask people for anything. If there is a choice between a man who is virtuous and a man who is wealthy, then the virtuous should be preferred."

(d) Wife is not to be treated casually. Quran says:

"And among His Signs is this that He created for you wives (spouses) from among yourselves, that you may find repose in them, and He has put between you affection and mercy. Verily, in that are indeed signs for people who reflect."

(Aayah No. 21, Surah Ar-Rum, Chapter No. 30, Holy Qur'an).

As a matter of fact Husband & Wife are screen for one another. Quran also says:

"They are libas (i.e. body cover, screen, dress) for you and you are the same for them."

(Aayah No. 187, Surah Al-Baqarah, Chapter No. 2, Holy Qur'an).

(e) The husband should give Mahr to his wife happily and without hesitation. Quran also says so:

"And give to the women their Mahr with a good heart; but if they, of their own good pleasure, remit any part of it to you, take it and enjoy it without fear of any harm."

(Aayah No. 4, Surah An-Nisa', Chapter No. 4, Holy Qur'an).

O you who believe! You are prohibited to inherit women against their will; and you should not treat them with harshness, that you may take away part of the Mahr you have given them, unless they commit open illegal sex; and live with them honourably. If you dislike them, it may be that you dislike a thing and Allah brings through it a great deal of good."

(Aayah No. 4, Surah An-Nisa', Chapter No. 4, Holy Qur'an).

(f) It is the duty of the husband to maintain his wife properly and provide him full protection as per religious dictates. The world and all things in it are valuable; but the most valuable thing in the world is a virtuous woman.

The virtuous wife is like the most precious pearl and the real wealth and she deserves to be treated and protected as such.

"Men are the protectors and maintainers of women, because Allah has made one of them to excel the other, and because they spend from their means." (Aayah No. 34, Surah An-Nisa', Chapter No. 4, Holy Qur'an).

In the present day human resource terminology, husband is the care-taker of his wife. It does not mean that men have a higher status over women. Fact of the matter is that Allah has made one of them to excel the other. Islam never promoted male chauvinism. It speaks of harmonious relationship between husband and wife based on mutual understanding and relative equality. It is one of the basic teachings of Islam that Muslims should follow a balanced path. Going to extremes without cogent reasons is not permissible in Islam.

(g) A good husband should avoid anger as Quran and our Prophet have expected from us:

Anger is able to destroy lives and relationships and Prophet Muhammad called it a hot coal on the heart of a descendant of Adam.[[1] At Tirmidhi] The Prophet said, "If anyone suppresses anger when he is in a position to give vent to it, God, the exalted, will call him on the Day of Resurrection and ask him to choose from the rewards offered."[[2] Abu Dawood] He also said, "No one has swallowed back anything more excellent in the sight of God, who is Great and Glorious, than anger, seeking to please God."[[3] At Tirmidhi]

Once a man came to Prophet Muhammad and said, "Messenger of God, teaches me some words which I can live by. Do not make them too much for me, in case I forget." He said, "Do not be angry."[[4] Saheeh Al-Bukhari] We find many instances of how to behave when we are in the midst of anger. He said, "If one of you becomes angry while standing he should sit down. If the anger leaves him, well and good; otherwise he should lie down".[At Tirmidhi] The Prophet also advised: "Anger comes from Satan, Satan was created from fire, and fire is extinguished only with water; so when any of you is angry, he should perform ablution".[Abu Dawood] Once Prophet Muhammad said to his companions, "I know words that if he were to say then his anger would go away, if he said, "I seek refuge with Allah from Satan," what he feels would go away."[Saheeh Al-Bukhari]

According to Imam Ahmad bin Hunbal, Prophet Muhammad had also advised that "If any of you becomes angry, let him keep silent." If a person is trying to be silent, it will obviously restrict his ability to fight or utter obscenities and harsh words. In another tradition Prophet Muhammad said: "If any of you becomes angry and he is standing, let him sit down, so his anger will go away; if it does not go away, let him lie down.

The Quran defines righteous people as,

"Those who spend (in God's Cause) in prosperity and in adversity, who repress anger, and who pardon the people; verily, God loves the good-doers." (Quran 3:134).

Prophet Muhammad's character is the practical example of utmost patience as his beloved wife Aisha said, 'His character was just (a reflection of) the Quran'.[Saheeh Muslim]

(h) The husband should maintain good personality to please his wife. Every good looking person or object looks good to one's eyes. This is the reason that we do not attend ceremonial functions in casual dress and go fully maintained so that we may look smart.

(i) The husband must be generous, soft spoken and accomodating. He must be a good listener and give full hearing and consideration to her grievances. While listening, one must not loose patience and should guard one's tongue. To err is human. The defaulter should be forgiven and her shortcomings overlooked. He should address his wife in the words she likes. Everyone wants to be praised and appreciated. One should avoid arguments on petty issues as it is not good to be argumentative all the times.

(j) The husband should call upon her to maintain good relations with his family and so the husband with her family.

(k) Exchange of gifts brings husband and wife closer. It is indicative of their love and affection for each other and strengthens their bond as spouse to each other, they being entitled to veneration or religious respect which is incumbent on them.

(l) If the wife reaches better heights in life, the husband should not feel jealous of her. Rather he should take it as his own achievement as her happiness is his happiness.

(m) The husband should help her wife in household work. It will not be out of place to mention here that some European countries have made it feasible by granting leave to the husbands to be the co-sharers of their wives in such activities.

(n) Be the co-sharer of your wife in child care as also in health care and general welfare of the family. Show the spirit of togetherness in all walks of life at and outside home. Taking food together and going for feasts together may bring husband and wife closer and turn them to be real bosom friends and life partners.

(o) The wives should also reciprocate the gestures of their husbands in the same spirit. They should please them with good manners, attractive dress, always smiling faces, affectionate welcome while coming back home from work and appreciate their achievements.

In an erratic situation they should not loose patience. They should sort out controversial matters in the manner ordained in Quran by way of mediation etc. In case of any default, the husband and wife should do introspection and try to assess objectively as who is at fault. They must take corrective steps and such things should never be the bone of contention between the two. They should maintain the same behaviour even in compelling situations. They should enjoy or share the hours of joy and sorrow, good and bad days, as the case may be, with each other.

All the attributes, contained in the above list, may be possessed only by a "made to order husband" but as many upright people have said, "Nothing is difficult when pursued for a right cause. All the attributes may not be relevant for Non-Muslims. It is very easy to give sermons but it is an uphill task to act upon. For a prospective Muslim wife, marrying a Muslim, the most important thing to look for in the man is that he should be a Muslim who adheres to all the laws and teachings of Islam in his daily life so that he may not take undue advantage of the liberal provisions in Muslim law, particularly in matters of marriage and divorce because a mere functional Muslim or a non-practicing Muslim may have no or scant regard for basic tenets of Islam and Quranic injunctions. The true believer shall never oppress or mistreat his wife or indulge in any act of domestic violence. However, it may not be assumed that only the believers treat their wives properly. Even those who have no interest in religious dictates and simply believe in ethical and moral values for being practiced in all walks of life, have been found to be responsible and dutiful husbands. The only difference between these two categories of persons is that the believers are more fearful and it is out of this fear that they behave responsibly even in abnormal situations.

Appendix 1

Terminology of Muslim Law

A

Adab: Good manners, etiquette, politeness, elegance of manners

Adl: Justice

AH: Anno Hegirae, beginning of Islamic calendar indicating the date when Prophet 'Muhammad (S) Left Mecca for Medina corresponding to 16th July, 622 (AD)

Ahad: None like God

Ahadees: Plural of Hadis which means Tradition or narration relating to or describing a saying or an action of Prophet Mohammad (S)

Ahkam: Orders, injunctions ordained in Qu'ran

Ahl-al-Bayt: People of the house, members of the Prophet Muhammad's Household (also known as Masumeen (innocent/ spiritually pure)

Ahlal-i-Kitab: Those who believe in a revealed religion—Muslims, Christians, Jews

Akhirat: Eternal life, next world

Akhlaq: Virtues, morals, morality, ethics

Allah: Allah is an Arabic word which means God in English, Ishwar in Hindi and Khuda in Persian and other equivalents in more than 2000 languages of the world, say, Dios in Spanish, Dio in Italian, Deus in Portuguese, Gott in German, Dumnezeu in Romanian, Dieu in French etc. God is one and one only. Other may be gods and devtas. They also command respect and reverence from their followers but at the same time those who do not believe in such gods and devtas they are also required to have full regard for their religious sanctity to their followers.

Alim: A scholar, a knowledgeful man, also a religious scholar or a theologist

Amanat: Trust, a thing or property committed to the trust and care of a person

Amin: Trustee, the person to whom a thing or property is given to keep it in trust and take care of it.

Amirul-Muminin: Commander of the faithful, a title assumed by the caliphs

Amr Bi'l Maruf: Islamic doctrine of encouraging others to move on the right track, the right way i.e. sirat-e-mustaqeem

Aqar: Landed property, immovable property

Aqd: Nikah, solemnisation of marriage according to Islamic rites

Aqidah: faith

Aqiqah: Islamic practice of shaving the head of the newborn and slaughtering an animal

Ashura: Tenth day of the month of Muharram

Assalamu Alaykum: The Islamic greeting which means "Peace be upon you" and wa-Rah.matulla-hi wa-Baraka-tuhu means "and the Mercy of God and His blessings"

Aslaf: Singular Salaf Predecessors/ancestors

Astana: Shrine, abode of a holy man, mausoleum

Atia: Grant, stipend, gratuity

Auqaf: Plural of waqf, Permanent dedication of immovable or movable property by a Muslim for a pious, religious or charitable cause

Aulad: Children

Azan: Call for paryer

B

Baatil: False, null and void

Baitullah: It means "house of God" that is Ka'aba at Makkah (Mecca)

Bakira: Virgin, unmarried

Baligh: Adult

Bashar: Man, mankind, humankind

Batin: Implied, the hidden, covert

Bidat: Novelty or innovation in religion

Bidati: The innovator, the wrong-doer

Baiat: Allegiance to a spiritual leader or a saint

Bulugh: Puberty

Burqa: Cover of cloth meant for covering the body

C

Caliph-khalifah: Successor of Prophet Muhammad (S)

D

Dahriya: Atheist

Dargah: Shrine or tomb of a reputed saint

Darul-Harb: Land of war, country of an enemy

Din: Often used to mean the faith and religion, Islam in the context of Muslim Law

Dua: Prayer

E

Eid-ul-Fitr-Id-ul-Fitr: The Festival of Fitr, that is, breaking the fast. It marks the end of Ramadan, the Islamic holy month of fasting

Eid-ul-Adha-Id-ul-Azha or Baqar'id: The Festival of Sacrifice in commemoration of Abraham's offering his son Ismail for sacrifice

F

Faqih: A theologist having a deep understanding of Islam, Islamic laws and jurisprudence

Farz: Obligatory religious duty

Fasid: Invalid, violable

Fasiq: One violating Islamic law

Fatiha: Commencement, the first chapter or exordium of the Qur'an that is, opening sura of the Qur'an, oblations and offerings to the deceased.

Fatwa: Opinion of a jurisconsult competent to give such opinion in matters relating to Muslim law

Fiqh: (Deep understanding and knowledge of) Muslim law and jurisprudence

G

Ghazi: A holy warrior, a mujahid fighting for a right cause

Ghusl: Bath

H

Hadis: (see ahadis)

Hafiz: Someone memorising Qur'an by heart

Hajj: Pilgrimage to Mecca

Haq: Right, truth, reality

Haram: Sinful, prohibited

Hijab: It means "cover". It is meant for covering the body. It has different names, such as, burqa, chadar, niqab, purdah etc.

Hijra (Hijri): Islamic era. It marks the begining of the Muslim New Year on the first day of the month of Muharram

Hikmah (Hikmat): Wisdom and understanding of the highest order

Hurmat: Honour, dignity, to be forbidden

I

Ibadat: Submission, worship

Idgah: Mosque for eid prayers

Iddat: The time of probation which a divorced woman or a widow must wait before she can marry again

Ijab: Proposal for marriage

Ijara: Letting land on lease

Ijtehad: Framing new rules based on sources of Islam to meet some new situation

Ijma: The unanimous authority, consensus of Muslim jurists on a point of law

Ila: To abstain from sexual intercourse for a period of not less than four months or for an unspecified period

Imam: One leading the prayer, successor of Prophet Muhammad(S) to act as leader of the masses

Imambara: Place for Moharram ceremonies

Iman: Personal faith, particularly in God, His words and apostles

Ikhlas: Sincerity, purity, loyalty, sincerity in religious beliefs (opposite of hypocricy)

Indattalab: Dower payable on demand

Inshaallah: God willing

Irtidad: Apostasy

Istishhad: Martyrdom

Istihsan: Framing new rules based on equity, fairness and justice

J

Ja'e-mukafat: Place of retribution, cause of retribution

Jaiz: Allowed or permissible (halal, that is, opposite of haram)

Jahannam: Hell

Jahiliyyah: Period of ignorance before Islam

Janamaz: Carpet, mat, piece of cloth for offering Namaz

Janazah: A bier with a corpse on it, a funeral

Jannah-Jannat: Paradise, Heaven

Jihad: Struggle, an earnest striving in the way of God only for a right and righteous cause exclusively against wrongdoers

Jinn: An invisible being of fire

Jizya: A tax to be paid by non-Muslims under Muslim rule for their foolproof protection

K

Kazi (Quazi): A religious person performing Nikah, a Muslim judge

Kalima: Confession of faith by a Muslim 'There is no God but God and Muhammad is the Prophet of God (Allah)

Kar-e-Khair: Charitable purpose

Khairat: Charity

Khanqah: monastery, a convent for sufi recluses

Khatib: A reciter of khutba

Khiar: Option, choice

Khiraj: A land tax

Khula: Dissolution of marriage at wife's instance

Khutba: Discourse, sermons

Kitabi: Those professing religion based on revealed books, such as, Christians, Muslims and Jews

Kitabia: A female professing religion based on revealed book

Kufu: Alike, parity between parties for matrimonial purposes

L

Lian: 1. Charge of Zina (Sexual intercourse outside matrimonial relationship) against wife 2. denial of the paternity of child 3. The husband may deny that wife was pregnant of him

M

Madrasah: School

Mahram: A relative of the opposite gender who can appear before the concerned person without observing purdah/hijab but can not marry him

Maher: Dower

Maher misl: Maher as per practice in the family

Makruh: It means "detested or disliked", though not haraam (forbidden)

Manasik: The rules specifying the requirements of a valid hajj

Maqbara: Tomb

Maraz-ul-maut: Mortal disease, death-illness

Mashaallah: What God wills

Masjid: Mosque

Masjid al-Haram: The mosque surrounding the Kabah in Mecca

Mazhab: Religion, belief, a body of tenets or articles of belief, school of law

Mecca: (Makkah) The holiest city in Islam, birth place of Prophet Muhammad(S)

Medina: (Madinah) A city in Saudi Arabia known as the City of the Prophet. It literally means "a city"

Moajjal: Prompt, to be paid immediately

Moakkil: Client

Millat: A nation, a community or the people

Minbar: A raised pulpit in the mosque where the Imam stands to deliver sermons

Muazzin: A person giving a call for prayer

Mubarat: Divorce by mutual agreement

Mufti: A Muslim scholar competent to issue fatwas

Muhammadur rasulullah: Muhammad(S) the Prophet and messenger of God

Mujawir: An attendant at a shrine

Mutabanna: Adopted child

Mutawalli: Mutawalli, Manager or supervisor of a waqf

Muwajjal: Deferred, to be paid later on

Muhajirin: The Muslims who accompanied Prophet Muhammad(S) when he travelled to Medina

Mujahid: A fighter for the faith only for a genuine cause

Mujtahid: A learned Islamic scholar

Mumin: A Muslim who observes the commandments of the Qur'an

Munafiq: Hypocrite, a dual personality

Murshid: Spiritual guide, a guide to the right way

Murtadd: apostate

Mushrik: A polytheist, One who associates others in worship of God

Muslim- Musalman: A follower of Islam. One who submits to Allah

Mutah: A temporary marriage, a pre-Islamic custom bearing resemblance and similarity to contemporary concept of live-in relationship

Mutawaffi: Deceased

N

Nabaligh: Minor

Nabi: The Prophet

Nafqa: Maintenance

Najaez: Invalid, unlawful, illegitimate

Najas: Impure

Nasab: Ancestry, pedigree

Nifaq: Hypocrisy, falsehood; dishonesty

Nikah: Contract of marriage between a Muslim bride and bridegroom

Nikahnama: Document containing contract of marriage between a Muslim bride and bridegroom

Niqab: Veil covering the face

P

Pardanashin: Veil covering woman

P.B.U.H.: An acronym that stands for "peace be upon him", a blessing which is affixed to Prophet Muhammad's name whenever it is written.

Prophet: A messenger of God

Q

Qabristan: Graveyard

Qadhf: False imputation of unchastity

Qiblah: The direction Muslims face during prayer, that is Ka'aba in Makkah

Qisas: Equitable retribution by way of pecuniary compensation if the heirs of the deceased forgive the perpetrator

Qiyas: Analogy – foundation of legal reasoning

Qubool: Acceptance

Quran: Qur'an (Koran) is the Holy divine book of Muslims revealed to prophet Muhammad(S) in 610 AD in the cave known as Hira by the angel Jibril.

Qurbani: Sacrifice, slaughtering of permissible animals on the occasion of Id -ul-Adha or on some ceremonial occasions

R

Rabb: God, Lord

Ramadan: Month of fasting

Rasul: (See Nabi)

Raza'at: Fostering

Raza'ee: Foster parents or sibling

Riba: Interest, usury

Risalat: Apostleship

Roza: Fast

Rusum: Customs and traditions

Ruh: Soul, spirit

Ruku: The bowing performed during salat (prayers)

S

Sadaqah: charity; voluntary alms

Sahabah: Companions of Prophet Muhammad(S)

Sajjadanashin: The spiritual superior of a religious endowment

Salat-Namaz: Sala(t) any one of the daily five obligatory prayers. The five obligatory prayers are:

1. Fajr: early morning prayer
2. Zohr: mid-day prayer
3. Asr: afternoon (generally between 4-30 p.m. and sunset) prayer
4. Maghrib: Evening (Sunset) prayer
5. Isha: The prayer at nightfall (generally after 8-30 p.m.)

Salam: Peace (see sulh), the greetings

Saum: Fasting during the month of Ramadan.

Sayed: A descendant of Prophet Muhammad. Literally, it is used like 'Mr', Shri.

Shaheed: Martyr

Sheikh: Muslim clergy, a caste (in the Indian context)

Shariat: The eternal ethical and moral code based on the Qur'an and Sunnah, Islamic code of law, The religious law of God (divine law) so believed by Muslims.

Shaitan: Satan, the Devil, also known as Iblis

Shiah: A Muslim sect

Shirk: Idolatry, polytheism

Shufa: Pre-emption

Shura: Consultation

Sirat: Life or biography of Prophet Muhammad(S)

Sirat-al-mustaqim: The Straight Path, the right path

Subah Sadiq: True dawn

Sufi: A Muslim mystic, one of a peculiar sect of Muslim devotees so called (they are said to be freethinkers or pantheists in matters of religion)

Seheri: The meal eaten by fasting Muslims just before dawn.

Sujud: Kneeling down during salat.

Sulh: A condition of peace

Sunnah or sunnat an-Nabi: The "path" or "example" of Prophet Muhammad(S), that is what the Prophet did, said or agreed to do during his life time.

Sunni: The largest denomination of Islam

Surah: Chapter of Qur'an

T

Taala: Almighty

Tabein: Followers of the Sahabah (companions of Prophet) Muhammad(S)

Tabniyat: Adoption

Tafsir: Commentary on the Qur'an

Tajdid: To purify and reform civil society

Tajdif: Blasphemy

Takbir: A proclamation of the greatness of Allah; a Muslim invocation

Takia: A place of repose, an abode of a faqeer (beggar), a place like a shrine or monastery

Talaq: Divorce

Talaq: Divorce, Kinds of

divorce in jest

divorce irrevocable

divorce, regular

divorce, reversible

divorce under coercion

divorce under intoxication

Taqwa: Righteousness, piety, preserving or guarding oneself from sin

Tasawwuf: or Sufism Mysticism, the theology of the Sufis

Tasbih: A string of beads for uttering words like "Subhan Allah" etc. to glorify and please Almighty Allah

Tawassul: Soliciting something from Allah Almighty through someone.

Tawaf: Circumambulating the Ka'bah during Hajj.

Taubah: Repentance

Tauhid: Monotheism; affirming Oneness of God (Allah) and accepting Muhammad His messenger.

Tayyib: All that is good, the most excellent

Tazia: Replica of Hazrat Imam Hussain's tomb

Tazir: Punishment

Thawab (Sawab): Reward for good deeds

Tuhr: Purity, cleanliness, menses free period of a woman

U

Ulema: Learned Islamic scholars

Ummah: The community of Muslim believers

Umrah: Unlike hajj, umrah can be performed throughout the year.

Urs: Ceremony for offerings and oblations to saints

Uqubah, uqubat: The branch of sharia that deals with punishment. (See hudud, qisas, tazeer)

V

Vakil: Lawyer, Representative, Person seeking permission of *nikah* from the bridegroom

Wa alaykum as-sala-m: Wa 'Alaykum as-Salaam!, meaning "and upon you be peace". (see As-Salamu Alaykum)

Wafat: Death

Wahdat al-wuju-d: "unity of being" a term used by some Sufis

Wahi: Revelation of God to His Prophets

Wajib: Necessary but not mandatory like farz

Wali: Guardian

Waris: Heir, successor

Wakf alal aulad: Family Waqf

Wakif: Author of the waqf deed, maker of a waqf

Waqf: See Auqaf

Wasi: Executor of a will

Wasiyat: Will

Wasilah: The means by which one achieves nearness to Allah

Wuzu: Ablution performed before prayers involving washing, first the hands, then the mouth inside, then throwing water on the forehead, washing the whole face, the arms and lastly the feet.

Y

Yawm ad-Din: Day of Reckoning

Yawm al-Qiya-mah: Day of Judgment

Z

Zaereen: Pilgrims or visitors to a shrine or mausoleum

Zabiha (Dhabi-h.ah): Islamic method of slaughtering an animal

Zaidi: Islamic sub-sect of Shias

Zakat: Alms to the poor of a portion or amount of a Muslim's property given by him/her as per religious dictates.

Zalimin: Polytheists, wrong-doers, and unjust.

Ziarat: A visit to a shrine or mausoleum, pilgrimage

Zihar: Pronouncing the words "Thou art to me like the back of my mother." It results in divorce.

Zina: Sexual intercourse outside matrimonial relationship

Zindiq: Heretic, atheist

Appendix 2

Marriage Sermon (Khutbah)

Khutbah is a discourse, sermon or oration which the khatib recites at the time of Nikah, an occasion for solemnisation of marriage. Khutbah Nikah is recited in Arabic. The wording differs from sect to sect and place to place because of followers of different schools of thought perform Nikah and recite Khutbah as per their convictions. But all the Khutbahs are generally based on what is ordained in Quran. Generally, the Khutbah contains the following sermons, being reproduced in English below:

Khutbah Nikah (In English)

"Thanks be to Allah that we praise Him, pray to Him for help; ask Him for pardon; we believe in Him, We trust Him; and ask Him to guard us from the evil of our own souls and from the evil consequences of our own deeds. Whomsoever He leaves straying no one can guide him. I bear witness that there is no God save Allah, who has no partner, and I bear witness that Muhammad is His servant and messenger, whom He has sent with truth as a bringer of good news and a warner.

Now, after Hamd-o-Salat, the best word is the book of Allah, and the best way is that of Muhammad, on whom be peace. Allah is an Arabic word which means god.

Whosoever obeys Allah and His messenger will be guided aright and whosoever disobeys will cause loss to his own self (and thereafter). Hereafter, I ask the refuge of Allah from Shaytan, the outcast.

O mankind! Be careful of your duty to your Lord who created you from a single soul and from it created its mate and from them twain hath spread abroad a multitude of men and women. Be careful of your duty towards Allah in whom you claim (your rights) of one another, and toward the wombs (that bear you). Lo, Allah hath been a watcher over you. [Surah Al Nisa' 4:1]

O ye who believe! Observe your duty to Allah with right observance, and die not save as those who have surrendered (unto Him). [Surah Ali 'Imran 3:102]

O ye who believe! Guard your duty to Allah, and speak words straight to the point; He will adjust your works for you and will forgive you, your sins. Whosoever obeyeth Allah and His messenger, he verily hath gained a signal victory. [Surah Al Ahzab 33:70-71]"

Appendix 3

The Dissolution of Muslim Marriages Act, 1939

An Act to consolidate and clarify the provisions of Muslim law relating to suits for dissolution of marriage by women married under Muslim law and to remove doubts as to the effect of the renunciation of Islam by a married Muslim woman on her marriage tie.

Whereas it is expedient to consolidate and clarify the provisions of Muslim law relating to suit for dissolution of marriage by women married under Muslim law and to remove doubts as to the effect of the renunciation of Islam by a married Muslim woman on her marriage tie; It is hereby enacted as follows:

1. Short title and extent. - (1) This Act may be called the Dissolution of Muslim Marriages Act, 1939;

(2) It extends to the whole of India except Part 'B' States.

2. Grounds for decree for dissolution of marriage—A woman married under Muslim law shall be entitled to obtain a decree for the dissolution of her marriage on any one or more of the following grounds, namely:

(i) That the whereabouts of the husband have not been known for a period of four years;

(ii) That the husband has neglected or has failed to provide for her maintenance for a period of two years;

(iii) That the husband has been sentenced to imprisonment for a period of seven years or upwards;

(iv) That the husband has failed to perform, without reasonable cause, his marital obligations for a period of three years;

(v) That the husband was impotent at the time of the marriage and continues to be so;

(vi) That the husband has been insane for a period of two years or is suffering from leprosy or a virulent venereal disease;

(vii) That she, having been given in marriage by her father or other guardian before she attained the age of fifteen years, repudiated the marriage before attaining the age of eighteen years:

Provided that the marriage has not been consummated;

(viii) That the husband treats her with cruelty, that is to say,–

(a) habitually assaults her or makes her life miserable by cruelty of conduct even if such conduct does not amount to physical ill-treatment, or

(b) associates with women of evil repute or leads an infamous life, or

(c) attempts to force her to lead an immoral life, or

(d) disposes of her property or prevents her exercising her legal rights over it, or

(e) obstructs her in the observance of her religious profession or practice, or

(f) if he has more wives than one, does not treat her equitably in accordance with the injunctions of the Quran;

(ix) on any other ground which is recognised as valid for the dissolution of marriages under Muslim law:

Provided that–

(a) no decree shall be passed on ground (iii) until the sentence has become final;

(b) a decree passed on ground (i) shall not take effect for a period of six months from the date of such decree, and if the husband appears either in person or through an authorised agent within that period and satisfied the Court that he is prepared to perform his conjugal duties, the Court shall set aside the said decree; and

(c) before passing a decree on ground (v) the Court shall, on application by the husband, made an order requiring the husband to satisfy the Court within a period of one year from the date of such order that he has ceased to be impotent, and if the husband so satisfies the Court within such period, no decree shall be passed on the said ground.

3. Notice to be served on heirs of the husband, when the husband's whereabouts are not known.—In a suit to which clause (i) of Section 2 applies—

(a) the names and addresses of the persons who would have been the heirs of the husband under Muslim law if he had died on the date of the filing of the plaint shall be stated in the plaint,

(b) notice of the suit shall be served on such persons, and

(c) such persons shall have the right to be heard in the suit:

Provided that paternal uncle and brother of the husband, if any, shall be cited as party even if he or they are not heirs.

4. Effect of conversion to another faith? The renunciation of Islam by a married Muslim woman or her conversion to a faith other than Islam shall not be itself operate to dissolve her marriage:

Provided that after such renunciation, or conversion, the woman shall be entitled to obtain a decree for the dissolution of her marriage on any of the grounds mentioned in Section 2:

Provided further that the provisions of this section shall not apply to a woman converted to Islam from some other faith who re-embraces her former faith.

5. Rights to dower not to be affected. ? Nothing contained in this Act shall affect any right which a married woman may have under Muslim law to her dower or any part thereof on the dissolution of her marriage.

6. [Repeal of Section 5 of Act 26 of 1937. Rep. by the Repealing and Amending Act, 1942 (25 of 1942)].

Appendix 4

The Muslim Personal Law (Shariat) Application Act, 1937

(ACT No. 26 OF 1937)

[7th October, 1937]

An Act to make provision for the application of the Muslim Personal Law (Shariat) to Muslims

Whereas it is expedient to make provision for the application of the Muslim Personal Law (Shariat) to Muslims; It is hereby enacted as follows:—

1. Short title and extent.

1. Short title and extent—(1) This Act may be called the Muslim Personal Law (Shariat) Application Act, 1937;

(2) It extends to the whole of India except the territories which, immediately before the 1st November, 1956, were comprised in Part 'B' States.

2. Application of Personal Law to Muslims.

Notwithstanding any customs or usage to the contrary, in all questions (save questions relating to agricultural land) regarding intestate succession, special property of females, including personal property inherited or obtained under contract or gift or any other provision of Personal Law, marriage, dissolution of marriage, including talaq, ila, zihar, lian, khula and mubaraat, maintenance, dower, guardianship, gifts, trusts and trust properties, and wakfs (other than charities and charitable institutions and charitable and religion endowments) the rule of decision in cases where the parties are Muslims shall be the Muslim Personal Law (Shariat).

3. Power to make a declaration.

3. (1) Power to make a declaration—Any person who satisfies the prescribed authority—

(a) that he is a Muslim, and

(b) that, he is competent to contract within the meaning of Section 11 the Indian Contract Act, 1872 (9 of 1872), and

(c) that he is a resident of the territories to which this Act extends, may by declaration in the prescribed form and filed before the prescribed authority declare that he desires to obtain the benefit of the provisions of this section, and thereafter the provisions of Section 2 shall apply to the declarant and all his minor children and their descendants as if in addition to the matters enumerated therein adoption, wills and legacies were also specified.

(2) Where the prescribed authority refuses to accept a declaration under sub-section (1), the person desiring to make the same may appeal to such officer as the State Government may, by general or special order, appoint in this behalf, and such officer may, if he is satisfied that the appellant is entitled to make the declaration, order the prescribed authority to accept the same.

4. Rule-making power.

4. (1) Rule-making power—The State Government may make rules to carry into effect the purposes of this Act.

(2) In particular and without prejudice to the generality of the foregoing powers, such rules may provide for all or any of the following matters, namely:-

(a) for prescribing the authority before whom and the form in which declarations under this Act shall be made;

(b) for prescribing the fees to be paid for the filing of declarations and for the attendance at private residences of any person in the discharge of his duties under this Act; and for prescribing the times at which such fees shall be payable and the manner in which they shall be levied.

(3) Rules made under the provisions of this section shall be published in the Official Gazette and shall thereupon have effect as if enacted in this Act.

(4) Every rule made by the State Government under this Act shall be laid, as soon as it is made, before the State legislature.]

5. Dissolution of marriage by Court in certain circumstances—Rep. by the Dissolution of Muslim Marriages Act, 1939 (8 of 1939), Section 6.

6. Repeals.

Appendix 5

The Muslim Women (Protection of Rights on Divorce) Act, 1986

[Act No. 25 of 1986 dated 19th May, 1986]

An Act to protect the rights of Muslim women who have been divorced by, or have obtained divorce from their husbands and to provide for matters connected therewith or incidental thereto. Be it enacted by Parliament in the Thirty-seventh year of the Republic of India as follows:-

1. Short title and extent

(1) This Act may be called the Muslim Women (Protection of Rights on Divorce) Act, 1986.

(2) It extends to the whole of India except the State of Jammu and Kashmir.

2. Definitions

In this Act, unless the context otherwise requires,-

(a) ~divorced woman~ means a Muslim woman who was married according to Muslim law, and has been divorced by, or has obtained divorce from, her husband in accordance with Muslim law;

(b) ~iddat period~ means, in the case of a divorced woman,-

(i) three menstrual courses after the date of divorce, if she is subject to menstruation;

(ii) three lunar months after her divorce, if she is not subject to menstruation; and

(iii) if she is enceinte at the time of her divorce, the period between the divorce and the delivery of her child or the termination of her pregnancy, whichever is earlier;

(c) ~Magistrate~ means a Magistrate of the First class exercising jurisdiction under the Code of Criminal Procedure Act, 1973 in the area where the divorced woman resides;

(d) ~prescribed~ means prescribed by rules made under this Act.

3. Mahr or other properties of Muslim woman to be given to her at the time of divorce

(1) Notwithstanding anything contained in any other law for the time being in force, a divorced woman shall be entitled to—

(a) a reasonable and fair provision and maintenance to be made and paid to her within the iddat period by her former husband;

(b) where she herself maintains the children born to her before or after her divorce, a reasonable and fair provision and maintenance to be made and paid by her former husband for a period of two years from the respective dates of birth of such children;

(c) an amount equal to the sum of *mahr* or dower agreed to be paid to her at the time of her marriage or at any time thereafter according to Muslim law; and

(d) all the properties given to her before or at the time of marriage or after her marriage by her relatives or friends or the husband or any relatives of the husband or his friends.

(2) Where a reasonable and fair provision and maintenance or the amount of *mahr* or dower due has not been made or paid or the properties referred to in clause (d) of sub-section—(1) have not been delivered to a divorced woman on her divorce, she or any one duly authorised by her may, on her behalf, make an application to a Magistrate for an order for payment of such provision and

maintenance, *mahr* or dower or the delivery of properties, as the case may be.

(3) Where an application has been made under sub-section (2) by a divorced woman, the Magistrate may, if he is satisfied that—

(a) her husband having sufficient means, has failed or neglected to make or pay her within the iddat period a reasonable and fair provision and maintenance for her and the children; or

(b) the amount equal to the sum of *mahr* or dower has not been paid or that the properties referred to in clause (d) of sub-section (1) have not been delivered to her, make an order, within one month of the date of the filing of the application, directing her former husband to pay such reasonable and fair provision and maintenance to the divorced woman as he may determine as fit and proper having regard to the needs of the divorced woman, the standard of life enjoyed by her during her marriage and the means of her former husband or, as the case may be, for the payment of such *mahr* or dower or the delivery of such properties referred to in clause (d) of sub-section (1) to the divorced woman:

Provided that if the Magistrate finds it impracticable to dispose of the application within the said period, he may, for reasons to be recorded by him, dispose of the application after the said period.

(4) If any person against whom an order has been made under sub-section (3) fails without sufficient cause to comply with the order, the Magistrate may issue a warrant for levying the amount of maintenance or *mahr* or dower due in the manner provided for levying fines under the Code of Criminal Procedure, 1973, and may sentence such person, for the whole or part of any amount remaining unpaid after the execution of the warrant, to imprisonment for a term which may extend to one year or until payment if sooner made, subject to such person being heard in defence and the said sentence 5 being imposed according to the provisions of the said Code.

4. Order for payment of maintenance

(1) Notwithstanding anything contained in the foregoing provisions of this Act or in any other law for the time being in force,

where a Magistrate is satisfied that a divorced woman has not re-married and is not able to maintain herself after the iddat period, he may make an order directing such of her relatives as would be entitled to inherit her property on her death according to Muslim law to pay such reasonable and fair maintenance to her as he may determine fit and proper, having regard to the needs of the divorced woman, the standard of life enjoyed by her during her marriage and the means of such relatives and such maintenance shall be payable by such relatives in the proportions in which they would inherit her property and at such periods as he may specify in his order:

Provided that where such divorced woman has children, the Magistrate shall order only such children to pay maintenance to her, and in the event of any such children being unable to pay such maintenance, the Magistrate shall order the parents of such divorced woman to pay maintenance to her:

Provided further that if any of the parents is unable to pay his or her share of the maintenance ordered by the Magistrate on the ground of his or her not having the means to pay the same, the Magistrate may, on proof of such inability being furnished to him, order that the share of such relatives in the maintenance ordered by him be paid by such of the other relatives as may appear to the Magistrate to have the means of paying the same in such proportions as the Magistrate may think fit to order.

(2) Where a divorced woman is unable to maintain herself and she has no relatives as mentioned in sub-section (1) or such relatives or any one of them have not enough means to pay the maintenance ordered by the Magistrate or the other relatives have not the means to pay the shares of those relatives whose shares have been ordered by the Magistrate to be paid by such other relatives under the second proviso to sub-section (1), the Magistrate may, by order, direct the State Wakf Board established under section 9 of the Wakf Act, 1954, or under any other law for the time being in force in a State, functioning in the area in which the woman resides, to pay such maintenance as determined by him under sub-section (1) or, as the case may be, to pay the shares of such of the relatives who are unable to pay, at such periods as he may specify in his order.

5. Option to be governed by the provisions of Sections 125 to 128 of Act 2 of 1974

If on the date of the first hearing of the application under Sub-Section (2) of Section 3, a divorced woman and her former husband declare, by affidavit or any other declaration in writing in such form as may be prescribed, either jointly or separately, that they would prefer to be governed by the provisions of Sections 125 to 128 of the Code of Criminal Procedure Act, 1973, and file such affidavit or declaration in the court hearing the application, the Magistrate shall dispose of such application accordingly.

Explanation,—For the purposes of this section, ~date of the first hearing of the application~ means the date fixed in the summons for the attendance of the respondent to the application.

6. Power to make rules

(1) The Central Government may, by notification in the Official Gazette, make rules or carrying out the purposes of this Act.

(2) In particular and without prejudice to the foregoing power, such rules may provide for—

- (a) the form of the affidavit or other declaration in writing to be filed under Section 5;
- (b) the procedure to be followed by the Magistrate in disposing of applications under this Act, including the serving of notices to the parties to such applications, dates of hearing of such applications and other matters;
- (c) any other matter which is required to be or may be prescribed.

(3) Every rule made under this Act shall be laid, as soon as may be after it is made, before each House of Parliament, while it is in session, for a total period of thirty days which may be comprised in one session or in two or more successive sessions, and if, before the expiry of the session immediately following the session or the successive sessions aforesaid, both Houses agree in making any modification in the rule or both Houses agree that the rule should not be made, the rule shall thereafter have effect only in such modified

form or be of no effect, as the case may be; so, however, that any such modification or annulment shall be without prejudice to the validity of anything previously done under that rule.

7. Transitional provisions

Every application by a divorced woman under Section 125 or under Section 127 of the Code of Criminal Procedure, 1973 pending before a Magistrate on the commencement of this Act, shall, notwithstanding anything contained in that Code and subject to the provisions of Section 5 of this Act, be disposed of by such Magistrate in accordance with the provisions of this Act.

List of Books Referred and Consulted

(Some books also referred in the text)

Quran

Ahadis (a traditions or narrations relating to or describing sayings or actions of the Prophet)

Abdur Rahim

Principles of Mohammedan Jurisprudence

Ameer Ali

Mohammedan Law, Vol. I

Mohammedan Law, Vol. II

Baillie

Neil, B.E.: Digest of Mohammedan Law. Part I & Part II

Dayal B.M.

The Darul Mukhtar

Fayzee A. A. A.

Outlines of Mohammedan Law

Hamilton

Translation of Hedaya (Grady's edition)

Hitti

History of Arabs (1953)

Howard, E.C.

Minhaj-et-talibin

Jungm M.U.

The Muslim Law of marriage.

The Muslim Law of Inheritance (containing translation of Sirajiyyah) (1964).

V.R. Krishna Iyer former Judge, Supreme Court of India and Recipient of Padma Vibhushan

The Dialectics & Dynamics of Human Rights in India (Yesterday, Today and Tomorrow) 1999

Lammens, H.

Islam : Beliefs and Institutions (English translation by Sir Denison Ross) 1929

Macdonald, D. B.

Development of Muslim Theology, Jurisprudence and Constitutional Theory (1903)

Macnaghten, Sir W. H.

Principles and Precedents of Mohammedan Law (Sloan's edition), 1897.

AL-HAJ MAHOMED ULLAH Ibn S. JUNG, M. A., LL.D. of Christ's College Cambridge; Barrister-at-Law, Lincoln's Inn, and High Court of Allahabad; Professor of Law at the University of Allahabad

The Muslim Law of Marriage

Sir William Markby, K.C.I.E., D.C.L.

Hindu and Mahommedan Law (1977) reprint

Mulla. Sir D.F.

Principles of Mohammedan Law

Rumsey. Almaric

Al-sirajiyyah or the Mohammedan Law of Inheritance (reprint from the translation of Sir William Jones). 2nd edition, 1890, cited as Siraj, (Rumsey)].

Sircar, S.C.

Tagore Law lectures, 1873.

Tagore Law lectures, 1874.

Tahir Mahmood & Saif Mahmood

Muslim Law in India and Abroad

Tyabji, F.B.
Mohammedan Law
Tyabji Kamila
Limited Interests in Mohammedan Law
Wilson, Sir R.K.
Anglo-Mohammedan Law
Encyclopaedia Britannica
B.R. Verma's
Commentaries on Mohammedan Law

Index

U

V

W

Z